AFTER THE REVOLUTION

After the Revolution

Waking to Global Capitalism

ARIF DIRLIK

Wesleyan University Press
Published by University Press of New England
Hanover and London

To the Memory of Lloyd E. Eastman

Wesleyan University Press
Published by University Press of New England, Hanover, NH 03755
© 1994 by Arif Dirlik
All rights reserved
Printed in the United States of America
5 4 3 2 1
CIP data appear at the end of the book

CONTENTS

PREFACE

This extended essay reflects on the theoretical and political implications of changes in the world situation over the last decade,
but especially since 1989. When in 1991 I began to delve systemati-
cally into the proliferating new literature on Global Capitalism, it
was with the limited—and exclusively personal—goal of making
some sense of the new world disorder. As I put down the thoughts
elicited by these readings, I found that a whole series of questions
that I had been pondering for some time, ranging from questions
of everyday life to questions of abstract theory, found their way

into the writing. This essay is the product. What, and how much, sense these reflections make in the end, I am not prepared to say; they are as likely to frustrate as to illuminate. Various occasions on which I have discussed the issues raised in the essay, as well as readings by respected colleagues and friends, have assured me that what the essay has to offer has a relevance beyond the personal; the epigraphs may indicate how much the essay owes to others' thoughts on these questions, as well as the ways in which it may resonate with the basic concerns of the times. I can only hope that at a time of obscurantist ideological complacency in the face of all the evidence of widespread human dislocation and alienation, the issues raised here will provoke some thought even among those who may disagree with parts or all of the essay.

I owe a debt of gratitude to those who with their suggestions and/or enthusiastic responses have given support to the project, and stimulated my thinking in new directions; I probably would have been wiser to take more of their advice. I would like to name in particular Bruce Cumings, Fredric Jameson, Rebecca Karl, Saree Makdisi, Maurice Meisner, Masao Miyoshi, Donald Pease, Roxann Prazniak, Rob Wilson, Yu Keping, and Zhang Xudong. I would like also to acknowledge my debt to participants in various forums where these issues were discussed at some length: The Marxism and Society Seminar at Duke University, the Workshop on Critical Alternatives in Asia/Pacific Studies at the University of Wisconsin-Madison, a special seminar at the Marxism-Leninism Institute of the Chinese Communist Party Central Compilation and Translation Bureau, and an informal seminar of the Department of International Politics at Beijing University.

I sadly dedicate this volume to the memory of a friend, and fellow historian of China, Lloyd E. Eastman of the University of Illinois, who passed away prematurely as this manuscript was going into publication. A foremost historian of Republican China, Lloyd was a relentless scholar. His personal grace and unfinished projects will be much missed.

A.D.

Smart Bombs, Dumb People: The New World Order

The Gulf War in 1991 did not usher in a "new world order" or "the end of history"—except as cant. It did mark unambiguously the arrival of a new cognitive disorder. For all intents and purposes, the war was between smart bombs and dumb people. One side had the smart bombs, which did all the fighting, obviating the need for human participation except to push the buttons that sent the bombs on their way. The bombs then did the job, finding their targets with deadly accuracy. The other side had the dumb people, imprisoned in underground bunkers with little idea of what transpired beyond the ceilings of the bunkers, until it was too late and no longer mattered. They never got to fight either.

While literal devastation by the thousands was the price Iraqi soldiers paid for their cognitive confinement, the devastation was not theirs alone, nor was the cognitive blindness. That the bombs did the job for human beings was a cause for celebration in the United States, bringing with it a frightening moral turpitude. From the public relations men in the Pentagon to TV and print journalists to the public at large, the war was celebrated for having caused few casualties. The last real war the United States had fought on Third World soil had taken a heavy toll. That people should have felt tremendous relief that their spouses, children, or parents would be returning home nearly intact was understandable. But during that other war, which had been played out daily on TV screens, there had also been a surge of compassion for the devastation of the other side, a sentiment that brought the two sides together in acknowledgment of the common humanity of suffering. This time, the rhetoric was to drive them apart; it betrayed no cognition of the one to two hundred thousand Iraqis who lay dead on or under the ground, who were left out of statements about "very few" or "negligible" casualties. The Pentagon orchestrated the news to assure public indifference to the Other. I doubt that the orchestration made all the difference, however, since the bombs did the job before there could be any serious fighting. Compassion was benumbed by the sight of electronic traces making their way to targets, which, for all anyone could see, contained no human beings. On one occasion when the general in charge of directing the Pentagon's news campaign was asked about Iraqi casualties, he responded lackadaisically that "it was their own fault"—the impeccable logic of the frog in the well, with the moral sensibility of a storm trooper. More frightening, the audience nodded. That such a statement would not even stir moral indignation suggests that maybe the people here, too, had been rendered dumb by smart bombs.

The Third World and the First in the new world order! The Gulf War was symptomatic of changed global relationships in the age of flexible production. To the extent that Third World societies defeated the might of First World military power in earlier conflicts, they did so by guerilla warfare. In the Gulf War, thanks to the new technologies, it was the combined military forces of the First, Second, and Third Worlds that danced circles around the stationary forces of Iraq.

AFTER THE REVOLUTION

Walter Benjamin's Ninth Thesis on the Philosophy of History

A Klee painting named "Angelus Novus" shows an angel looking as though he is about to move away from something he is fixedly contemplating. His eyes are staring, his mouth is open, his wings are spread. This is how one pictures the angel of history. His face is turned toward the past. Where we perceive a chain of events, he sees a single catastrophe which keeps piling wreckage upon wreckage and hurls it in front of his feet. The angel would like to stay, awaken the dead, and make whole what has been smashed. But a storm is blowing from paradise; it has got caught in his wings with such violence that the angel can no longer close them. This storm irresistably propels him into the future to which his back is turned, while the pile of debris before him grows skyward. This storm is what we call progress.[*]

[*] Walter Benjamin, "Theses on History," in *Illuminations*, ed. by Hannah Arendt (New York: Harcourt, Brace and World, 1968), pp. 255–66.

On the first anniversary of the new world order, Senator Ernest Hollings (D-SC) suggested that we send to Japan a picture of a mushroom cloud with the inscription, "Made in the USA, tested in Japan." Senator Hollings later said that it had been a joke. Welcome to the new world order.

I

Whither Marxism?

Any consideration of radical possibilities in our day must begin with a critique of Marxism. For the past century and a half, Marxism has provided the most fundamental criticism of capitalist society. It has also served as the inspiration for the various socialisms that have held forth the only plausible challenge to capitalism in the alternative modes of social and economic organization they have proffered.

For all practical purposes, socialist societies are no more, which faces Marxism with an unprecedented crisis, and raises the question of the part Marxism may have to play in formulating radical options for the future. The necessity of radical options is not in question; the contemporary crisis is not just a crisis of socialism or Marxism but a crisis of capitalism as well, which we manage to avoid noticing by wallowing in crises as a condition of daily life now that there seem to be no alternatives to capitalism. Sooner or later there will have to be. The question is how to conceive of such options at a time when the foremost source of alternatives to capitalism seems to have disintegrated under the weight of its own historical consequences.

The ability of capitalism to survive the many crises that have marked its history has repeatedly called into question the validity of the Marxist argument. Marxism has also been questioned from alternative radical perspectives by those who have felt that, in its almost single-minded preoccupation with economic exploitation and the question of class, Marxism has been blind to problems of oppression and exploitation that have their sources outside of a narrowly conceived economic organization under capitalism. These questions acquired momentum over the last few decades as it became apparent that while socialist societies had been able to resolve some questions of economic exploitation and oppression, they left unresolved other fundamental social and political problems which, if anything, appeared in these societies with even greater sharpness than they did in capitalist societies.

Such questions, in their persistence, have disillusioned and demoralized generation after generation of Marxists. As long as socialist societies could claim to offer viable alternatives to capitalism, however, it has been possible for Marxists to avoid questioning the fundamentals of Marxism by holding forth the promise of future solutions to present problems. Now that the fall of socialist societies has seemingly deprived Marxism of a future, it is no longer possible to postpone to the future a confrontation of these problems. Radical changes in global economic organization have not only played a part in the demise of socialist societies but have also called into question the continued relevance of Marxism. The emergence of Global Capitalism, which moved into the foreground with the collapse of socialist societies, has remapped the relationship of societies to one another, has altered the role of nation-states, and has created a need to reconsider all critical perspectives of development and social change. While the major social constituency of Marxist theory, the working class, has been relegated to a secondary social significance with these changes, other constituencies have come forward to stake their claims on politics and the future of society. While declarations of the demise of Marxism may be premature, therefore, it is quite clear that Marxism is no longer sufficient to account for the problems of a new world situation. The vision of human liberation, broadly conceived as liberation from economic want and social and political exploitation and oppression, must be grounded now in a world situation that is worlds apart from that in Marx's time, and must incorporate the visions of new social constituencies that have come forward with this new situation.

It is a new world situation that has created this most recent, albeit unprecedented, crisis of Marxism. This same world situation, however, has also brought to the surface features of capitalist development that, ironically, throw into relief fundamental premises of Marxism that account for its failures as a radical critique of capitalism. It is important at the present to confront these premises in all their nakedness if we are to grasp fully the shortcomings of the Marxist critique of capitalism and, given the centrality of Marxism to all radical theorizing, of radical formulations of alternatives to capitalism in the past. The goal here is not to reevaluate Marxism once again in the midst of another crisis of radicalism so as to rescue it from its own past. The goal is to bring these shortcomings to the surface so as to confront them squarely in the consideration of radical possibilities for the future, however remote the latter may seem.

In the following pages I discuss Marxism in relation to the contemporary reconfiguration of societies globally—the fall of socialist states and, most importantly, the emergence of Global Capitalism, which provides the broadest context for comprehending contemporary global transformations. Marxism is essential to grasping the nature and consequences of these transformations, I argue, but only insofar as it is freed from the modernizationism that is built into the theory. After all, what is at issue currently is not just Marxism but the whole notion of modernization and development (or "maldevelopment," as Vandana Shiva calls it). Just as Marxism needs to be freed from the spatial and temporal teleology of modernization, it needs also to be freed from conceptual teleology, to be opened up to alternative conceptualizations of social change, even if the result is compromising, or even abandoning, its integrity as theory. The question of liberation, I argue, is not to be contained by any one theory, including Marxism. If the theory must be compromised to achieve the goal of liberation, so be it, for theory exists to promote liberation, not to yoke the promise of liberation to its own sustenance, or to the sustenance of the particular vision that informs it.

My conclusions on forming an agenda of liberation appropriate to contemporary circumstances are not easily recognizable as Marxist; they are even likely to be viewed as anti-Marxist. I argue, in general, that the key categories of conventional Marxism (including the category of class) are not only insufficient for dealing with the problem of liberation but are also insufficient for grasping the full complexity of contemporary capitalism, of the social formations and problems it has generated or brought to the surface of consciousness globally. Therefore, I resist any theoretical totalization in terms of these categories and seek to open up Marxism to categories that are not implicit in Marxist theoretical formulations. My critique has as its point of departure the criticism of the metatheoretical spatial and temporal premises of Marxism, which is intended to historicize Marxism as a theory limited by its containment in the capitalist society that gave rise to it in the first place, and which also sets its boundaries as theory and vision. My argument thus concludes that the vision of liberation must be formulated independently of theory because it is not immanent in Marxism as proponents have assumed in the past; or, more accurately, that the vision that is immanent in the theory is limited by its origins in capitalist society.

I insist, however, that Marxist theory, and the revolutionary practices it has informed, are indispensable for grasping the conditions of this argument for "liberation from theory." My own formulations, in other words, would have been impossible without Marxist theory and the historical experience it has produced. My analysis of contemporary capitalism (and the fate within it of socialism) is informed by a Marxist analysis of capitalism, as is the world system theory in its various manifestations upon which I draw directly. Even the qualifications I introduce into the theory (into its categories as well as into its metatheoretical premises) are products of revolutionary experiences with Marxism. For insights into problems of theory I rely on the Chinese revolutionary experience of the 1930s, articulated fully in Maoist Marxism, which I take to be an instance of a Third World confrontation with Marxism. These qualifications are already part of a Marxist theoretical and revolutionary tradition, although Marxists perhaps have been reluctant to recognize their full implications.

What is at issue here is not a repudiation but a "self-criticism" of Marxism. I do repudiate totalizing procedures that render Marxism into a closed system which, in spite of their claims to totality, are guided by a categorical reductionism that sublates all other social categories into one or another Marxist category. Totalizing procedures are necessary to confront capitalism in its totality and, more importantly, to go beyond capitalism to incorporate problems of society and liberation that are not to be contained within the problematic of capitalism (and a Marxism that takes its cues from capitalism), regardless of how important capitalism may be in bringing such problems to the surface of consciousness. This alternative mode of totalizing, however, must be open-ended (which is to say, historical), rather than limited *a priori* by categorical presuppositions. This is not a simple pluralism, because it retains the aspiration to totality, and the necessity of articulating categories in the process of formulating totality *historically*; as it presupposes that social categories in their concrete manifestations appear not in isolation from one another, as they do in analytical abstraction, but in irreducible overdeterminedness which gives them their conjunctural meaning within historically changing totalities, as well as shaping the procedures by which such totalities are to be grasped. This also conditions my assertion here that the goals of liberation must be formulated independently of theory. Ethical choices that are not necessarily implicit in theory, or even in its immediate historical circumstances, are important in formulating those goals. This is not to say, however, that the choices are themselves arbitrary; whether or not they are possible, or even find their way into consciousness, the choices are not to be divorced from the material circumstances of liberation. Marxism has much to say in this regard as well. In order to remain true to its goals of liberation, however, this Marxism must redefine itself in the process of the struggle for liberation and be prepared to incorporate its conception of totality into even broader totalities that may appear on the horizon of such struggles and, ultimately, even to abolish itself as theory.

Let me illustrate these points by a few words on "class." I conclude later that the category of class, the central category of Marxist social analysis, is insufficient for analyzing the conditions of liberation and may even obstruct the task of liberation through its reductionism. This is not to say, however, that the concept of class is dispensable to social analysis or irrelevant in formulating the goals of liberation. Of all the categories that are presently current in radical social analysis (I am thinking of gender, ethnicity, race, etc.), class is the one category that is not reducible to concrete social identification. Its very abstractness is thus crucial to uncovering the social relationships that lie at the core of the capitalist mode of production, hidden from view in its everyday operations. Categories such as gender and ethnicity, however much we may insist that they are social constructs, nevertheless have readily identifiable social (and, in the extreme, biological) referents. Class does not, except as an abstraction that is deducible only within the system itself. The tentativeness historically of the concrete social manifestations of class provide ample testimonial to its abstractness, for such manifestations are contingent for their emergence not on any readily identifiable social ties but on the rather abstract notion of "class consciousness," which is easily overwhelmed in everyday life by more concrete social relationships. To use Marx's terminology, if class makes sense as a concept, it makes sense mainly "in-itself" rather than "for itself," which may be at the root of the historical failure of Marxism to generate and sustain a class-based politics. Even where class politics has generated class organization, there has been a tendency for the organization to divorce itself from its social constituency because the constituency fails to maintain solidarity on an ongoing basis.

This abstractness is, however, what makes class as a concept more, not less, important. To the extent that capitalism provides the systemic context even for problems that are not of its making (though it may be responsible for bringing them forward as problems and endowing them with their particular manifestations) the category of class cuts across all other categories of social analysis. *Because* it is most important not as a concrete social entity but as an abstract rational category, class enables a rational critique of capitalism in a way that competing concepts do not. It points to the fundamental principle for the organization of power in capitalist society; for power in capitalist society itself is abstract, the attribute of the operations of the system rather than of any exclusive social group. It is possible to imagine a capitalism that has assimilated different genders, ethnicities, and so on into its structure; it is not possible to imagine capitalism without classes. If these other categories are necessary to understand the concrete manifestations of class in political consciousness and activity, class itself is even more indispensable to the ideological demystification of these categories in the analysis of power. Because of their very social concreteness, genders, ethnicities, and other such categories are readily assimilable into the power structure of capitalist society, and it is relatively easy to mistake the assimilation of some members of the groups in question for the assimilation of the whole. Group identification comes much easier when the group appears as a concrete social entity.

The problem with class, on the other hand, is its reductionism, its assumption that the problems presented by all these other social relationships can be reduced to a problem of class because that is *the* problem of capitalist society. This reductionism, in my view, is where the horizon of Marxist theory (and vision) is limited by its context in capitalism and by its own abstract formulations concerning capitalism. Because class in its concrete manifestation never appears in a pure form but only in the overdetermined concreteness of social existence, to view it in isolation from other social categories is not only analytically misleading but is also an obstacle to the everyday struggle for liberation. The vision of the liberation itself is limited by collapsing into the problem of class these other problems that, not being exclusive problems of capitalist society, are likely to persist past capitalism—and have done so in the so-called socialist societies.

The unfolding of contemporary capitalism has brought these problems all the more insistently into the forefront of consciousness. The confrontation with the concrete, I argue later, points to the "borderlands" (of categories no less than of societies) as the locales for the struggles for liberation. The search becomes one not only for new ethical directions but also for more open-ended theoretical formulations because capitalism has brought the borderlands to the center of the problematic of liberation, as its immediate condition. Marxism as we have known it in the past is not sufficient to confront the full complexity of the borderlands, which is not to say that it does not have a crucially significant part to play in understanding them or in producing alternative futures. To do so, however, it has to liberate itself from its own limited horizons set by the capitalist mode of production from which the theory has historically arisen.

In the discussion here, I am concerned less with the specific theoretical formulations of Marxism than with its metatheoretical premises—specifically, its spatial and temporal premises. I have two reasons for taking this approach. First, I think that the theory's spatial and temporal premises (which are distinguishable analytically as long as we remember that they are but different aspects of the same procedure of conceptualization) hold sway over its theoretical formulations and, in a fundamental sense, shape the latter. Recent developments within capitalism have brought questions of space and time to the foreground in considerations of theory. I will return to these points in my conclusion, but I would like to suggest here that these questions have been apparent all along in "Third World" perspectives on Marxism. To illustrate the problems they present, I will take Chinese Marxism as my point of departure.

Second, I am concerned with these metatheoretical premises because I think they are of fundamental relevance to a crucial question that faces Marxism presently: What are the critical limits of Marxism? Stated somewhat differently, Is Marxism capable, conceptually, of transcending capitalist society, or is it limited in its critical capabilities by the boundaries of capitalism as mode of production *and* representation, and possibly even by a certain phase or certain aspects of capitalism? I will argue that, in its spatial and temporal premises, Marxism is indeed limited by a conceptualization of the world in which the capitalist mode of production provides the principles for ordering time and space or, as Immanual Wallerstein has put it, TimeSpace.[1] More bluntly, beneath the surface formulations concerning an alternative social existence to that prevailing under capitalism, Marxism in its spatial and temporal premises has suffered from the ideological hegemony of the capitalist mode of production of which it was the product, which has limited its ability to conceive of authentic alternatives to capitalism—to which the ruins of "socialist" societies stand as sad testimonials. For all its powerful critique of capitalism, therefore, Marxism must rise and fall with the capitalist mode of production. To state this is only to recall George Lukacs' description of Marxism (or, historical materialism) as "the self-knowledge of capitalist society."[2] I would like to go further here and suggest that, even within capitalist society, a critique that points beyond (or outside) the capitalist mode of production must of necessity transcend Marxism as well. This is not the same as saying that such a critique can afford to ignore what Marxism has to say about capitalism; on the contrary, I will argue that Marxism is essential, though not sufficient, to any thoroughgoing critique of the capitalist mode of production. It is even arguable that, liberated from the hold of its spatial and temporal premises, Marxism as critical theory may be able to transcend the boundaries of capitalism, though that may require the abolition of the theory *as* theory or, at the least, theory as we have known it. Here, once again, Chinese Marxism has some insights to offer, even if those insights were formulated only to be abandoned subsequently.

It should be abundantly clear from this formulation of the problem of Marxism that I do not subscribe to the currently fashionable view that the collapse of existing socialist societies implies the end of Marxism, not because I do not think there is a connection between Marxism and "actually existing socialism" but because Marxism is coeval with capitalism, not with existing socialist societies. I agree with Fredric Jameson when he writes of current views regarding the end of Marxism:

> The most hilarious incoherence, in my view, is the one that simultaneously proclaims the triumph of capitalism and the end of Marxism. But Marxism is first and foremost the study of capitalism and its specificities and contradictions: if capitalism is now universal (as Marx thought it had to be before socialism—which he considered to be structurally latent within capitalism—was conceivable), then surely Marxism is even more relevant than it was before.[3]

Jameson's statement on the "latency" of socialism within capitalism illustrates what I think may be problematic about Marxism, but otherwise he states cogently why Marxism may be more relevant today than ever before. Indeed, the fall of socialist states may have had a liberating consequence in releasing Marxism from its ties to existing socialist states. It is possible, for instance, that the new post-socialist environment has had something to do with the readiness with which today's politicians and public alike in the United States speak of socialized medicine, oppression of labor by capital, and a state that is in the service of the rich and powerful— all as part of a general acknowledgment of the crisis of capitalism—without fear of association with communism. Arguments over the 1992 federal budget were rife with charges of "promoting class warfare" and "class warfare of the rich against the poor." On the "McNeil/Lehrer Report" on 23 March 1992, Clarence Page, an editorial writer for the *Chicago Tribune*, commented that "1992 may be remembered as the year class came out of the closet in American politics." Now that socialism is dead, Marxism can return home to capitalist societies!

More significantly where theory is concerned, the fall of socialist states releases Marxism from ideological servitude to authoritarian bureaucracies and provides a new opportunity for theoretical consideration and development. As Paul Ricoeur has written:

> The creation of an official doctrine by the party provokes another phenomenon of ideology. . . . Just as religion is accused of having justified the power of the dominant class, so too Marxism functions as a system of justification for the power of the party as the avant-garde of the working class and for the power of the ruling group within the party. This justificatory function with respect to the power of a dominant group explains why the sclerosis of Marxism provides the most striking example of ideology in modern times. The paradox is that Marxism after Marx is the most extraordinary exemplification of his own conception of ideology as the sustained expression of the relation to reality and as the occultation of that relation.[4]

In my terms, now that Marxism has been released from the hegemony of bureaucratic states, it may be easier to confront the hegemony of capitalism within the premises of the theory and to consider further possibilities for its development. Indeed, the experience of existing socialist states has done much to reveal how the theory is distorted by these premises.

The problems presented to Marxism by the fall of existing socialist states are not theoretical but practical, which is not to say that they are therefore insignificant. The disillusionment with existing socialist experiments, accompanied by the apparent victory of capitalism over socialism, has made for a reluctance to speak for or to hear about Marxism. Few around the world today, unlike in earlier days, uphold a socialist model as a viable alternative to capitalism. In fact, the hegemony of capitalism appears to be more seamless than at any time in the past. While obviously discouraging to anyone who would speak about Marxism seriously, this situation neither implies that the crisis of capitalism has been resolved nor does it negate the importance of theory; rather, it calls for a reconsideration of theory from fresh perspectives that account for both the developments within capitalism and the histories of socialist states. The fall of socialist societies does not mean that Marxism is, therefore, dead. As long as the capitalist mode of production persists, Marxism, too, will retain its relevance—with or without Marxists. Those who are quick to declare the death of Marxism (from George Bush to China specialists)[5] on the evidence of the demise of socialist systems conveniently overlook that the bourgeois alternative to socialism in development theory, the idea of modernization, is itself in deep trouble, if not altogether meaningless, in spite of its apparent victory over socialism.

Indeed, the serious challenge to Marxism as theory is not the fall of existing socialist states but rather new developments within global capitalism. These developments, while playing a part in the downfall of socialist states, also rendered irrelevant previous approaches to development, including "modernization" itself. These changes have produced new conceptualizations of time and space that call into question basic premises of Marxist theory, themselves derivative of the spatial and temporal teleology of the capitalist mode of production. If Marxism meets its demise, it will be because of an inability or incapacity to accommodate these changes and to come to terms with alternative radical critiques of capitalist society that have their sources outside the Marxist tradition. In other words, can Marxism be made into something other than a "derivative discourse"—that is, derivative of capitalism?[6]

What is at issue, therefore, is the future, not present, relevance of Marxism. Because Marxism is crucial to any critique of capitalism, no consideration of the future can afford to overlook the critical premises within the theory. Marxism as a guide to the future, however, is another matter entirely from Marxism as a critique of capitalism. The Marxist vision of the future has been distorted by its internalization of capitalist spatiality and temporality; thus Marxism, as we have known it, however effective as a critique of capitalism, does not promise a viable or a desirable alternative to the capitalist mode of production. The fragmentation of capitalist spatiality and temporality with recent changes in global capitalism has undermined the spatial and temporal premises of Marxism and may free Marxism from the ties that historically have bound it to the capitalist mode of production. If so, the present crisis may offer new possibilities for reformulating a radical vision of society in which Marxism is essential, if only, in the words of Ricoeur, as "one working tool among others."[7]

Third World Utopianism

The Indian psychologist Ashis Nandy is a thinker of wisdom whose social philosophy draws upon Gandhi's legacy. Here are some of the things he has to say about "unthinking" modernity: *

Modernity is neither the end-state of all cultures nor the final word in institutional creativity. . . . One day there will have to be post-modern societies and a post-modern consciousness, and those societies and that consciousness may choose to build not so much upon modernity as on the traditions of the non-modern or pre-modern world [p. xvii]. . . . No dialogue is possible with a utopia claiming a monopoly on compassion and social realism. . . . Such a vision not merely devalues all heretics and outsiders as morally and cognitively inferior, it defines them as throw-backs to an earlier stage of culture and history. . . . Thus, if paganism is an early stage of monotheism, and ahistoricity that of historicity, the monotheists and the historically-minded cannot only claim to understand themselves and their world better than the primitives understand theirs, they can also claim to understand the primitives and their world better than the primitives do. Indeed, as historians to the world, the historically-minded can claim to know the future of the pagans and the ahistoricals better than the latter, for the future can be no different than the present of the civilized. Both the present and the future of the savage are thus hegemonized [p. 11]. . . . Human civilization is constantly trying to alter or expand its awareness of exploitation and oppression. . . . Who, before the socialists, had thought of class as a unit of oppression? How many, before Freud, had sensed that children needed to be protected against their own parents? How many believed, before Gandhi's rebirth after the environmental crisis in the West, that modern technology, the supposed liberator of man, had

* Ashis Nancy, *Traditions, Tyranny and Utopias: Essays in the Politics of Awareness* (Delhi: Oxford University Press, 1987).

become his most powerful oppressor? Our limited ethical sensitivity is not a proof of human situation. . . . Imperfect societies produce imperfect remedies of their imperfections. Theories of salvation are always soiled by the spatial and temporal roots of the theorists [p. 22]. . . . The fear of soft answers to hard questions is a fear of cultures which refuse to give an absolute value to hardness itself. . . . Vulgar materialism . . . is now an ally of the global structure of oppression. . . . In the name of shifting the debate to the real world, it reduces all choice to those available within a single culture, the culture affiliated to the dominant global system [pp. 23–25]. . . . The aim of the oppressed should be, not to become a first-class citizen in the world of oppression instead of a second or third class one, but to build an alternative world where he can hope to win back his humanity [p. 34]. . . . The peripheries of the world often feel that they are victimized not merely by partial, biased or ethnocentric history, but by the idea of history itself. . . . The more scientific a history, the more oppressive it tends to be in the experimental laboratory called the third world. . . . Even the histories of oppression and the historical theories of liberation postulate stages of growth which, instead of widening the victims' options, reduce them [pp. 46–48]. . . . As the peripheries of the world have been subjected to economic degradation and political impotency and robbed of their human dignity with the help of dionysian theories of progress, the first and the second worlds too have sunk deeper into intellectual provincialism, cultural decadence and moral degradation. . . . [All this is not] an elaborate attempt to project the sensitivities of the third world as the future consciousness of the globe or a plea to the first world to wallow in a comforting sense of guilt. Rather, it is a matter of admitting that while each civilization must find its own authentic vision of the future and its own authenticity in the future, neither is conceivable without admitting the experience of co-suffering which has now brought some of the major civilizations of the world close together. It is this co-suffering which makes the idea of cultural closeness something more than the chilling concept of One World which nineteenth century European optimism popularized and promoted to the status of a dogma [pp. 52–54].

The French thinker Roger Garaudy writes: "Occident is an accident. For the first time in human history, since what the occidentals call their 'renaissance'—that is, the simultaneous birth of capitalism and colonialism—science has been separated from wisdom and a technique has developed for techniques." *

*Nandy, Traditions, Tyranny and Utopias, Preface, p. ix.

2

The Marxist Narrative of Development and Chinese Marxism

> The bourgeoisie, by the rapid improvement of all instruments of production, by the immensely facilitated means of communication, draws all, even the most barbarian, nations into civilisation. The cheap prices of its commodities are the heavy artillery with which it batters down all Chinese walls, with which it forces the barbarians' intensely obstinate hatred of foreigners to capitulate. It compels all nations, on pain of extinction, to adopt the bourgeois mode of production; it compels them to introduce what it calls civilisation into their midst, i.e., to become bourgeois themselves. In one word, it creates a world after its own image.[8]

Although global development has taken a tortuous course since 1848 when Marx and Engels penned these lines, and though even Marx's closest followers have had to qualify some of his observations on the impact of the bourgeoisie on the world, few would quarrel with his description of the global impact of the capitalist mode of production. There was more resistance than Marx anticipated, including the resistance inspired by his own ideas, that prolonged the process (and that still goes on); but that such a process has been at work since Marx's day is hardly questionable—least of all by the bourgeoisie who finally feel confident enough to proclaim the victory of capitalism and the end of history.

What is of interest here are the spatial and temporal presumptions of this narrative of capitalism. The bourgeois mode of production, according to Marx and Engels, homogenizes space within individual societies and globally, literally and metaphorically, by tearing down all "Chinese walls," by overrunning all alternative modes of production, by abolishing all differences in social space defined by class, occupation, and even kinship:

> In the earlier epochs of history, we find almost everywhere a complicated arrangement of society into various orders, a manifold gradation of social rank. . . . The epoch of the bourgeoisie, possesses, however, this distinctive feature: it has simplified class antagonisms. Society as a whole is more and more splitting up into two great hostile camps, into two great classes directly facing each other: Bourgeoisie and Proletariat. . . . The bourgeoisie has stripped of its halo every occupation hitherto honoured and looked up to with reverent awe. It has converted the physician, the lawyer, the priest, the poet, the man of science, into its paid wage-labourers. The bourgeoisie has torn away from the family its sentimental veil, and has reduced the family relation to a mere money relation. . . . The bourgeoisie has through its exploitation of the world-market given a cosmopolitan character to production and consumption in every country. . . . In place of the old local and national seclusion and self-sufficiency, we have intercourse in every direction, universal interdependence of nations. And as in material, so also in intellectual production. The intellectual creations of individual nations become common property. National one-sidedness and narrow-mindedness become more and more impossible, and from the numerous national and local literatures, there arises a world literature. . . . The bourgeoisie has subjected the country to the rule of the towns. It has created enormous cities, has greatly increased the urban population as compared with the rural, and has thus rescued a considerable part of the population from the idiocy of rural life. Just as it has made the country dependent on the towns, so it has made barbarian and semi-barbarian countries dependent on the civilised ones, nations of peasants on nations of bourgeois, the East on the West.[9]

Implicit in this homogenization of space is the globalization of time, where local histories are incorporated into national histories that, in turn, become part of a world history. The bourgeoisie that was in the process of creating this world history was in a basic sense a truly historical class, because whereas "the conservation of the old modes of production in unaltered form was . . . the first condition of existence for all earlier industrial classes," the bourgeoisie could not "exist without constantly revolutionising the instruments of production, and thereby the relations of production, and with them the whole relations of society." [10] By implication, the only true history was that which had brought this class into existence, against which other societies appeared, as Marx put it in another context, merely to be "vegetating in the teeth of time." [11] The bourgeoisie, in other words, was not merely the creator of world history; its history also provided the criterion of temporality against which other pasts must be judged. In contrast to the dynamism of the bourgeois epoch, to take one example, in Indian society, Marx observed,

> The simplicity of the organization for production in . . . self-sufficing communities that constantly reproduce themselves in the same form, and if destroyed, by change, spring up again on the same spot and with the same name—this simplicity supplies the key to the secret of the *unchangeableness* of Asiatic *societies*, an unchangeableness in such striking contrast with the constant dissolution and refounding of Asiatic *States*, and the never-ceasing changes of dynasty. The structure of the economic elements of society remains untouched by the storm-clouds of the political sky.[12] (emphasis in the original)

The bourgeoisie was not only the first truly historical class but, in creating world history, performed the historical function of compelling into history these unchanging and "unchangeable" societies. It goes without saying that these societies entered history not as subjects but as objects of the transformative powers of capitalism.

I have quoted the well-known lines from the *Communist Manifesto* at length because the rhetoric is relevant to the argument here. Robert Tucker has described the *Communist Manifesto* as "a compressed summary of the Marxian theory of history." [13] In other words, while Marx's account of the rise of the bourgeoisie and its impact on the world is descriptive, the description becomes part of a theory, and, through the intermediation of theoretical abstraction, acquires a nomological status. The rhetoric indicates the normative significance with which Marx endowed the rise of capitalism. In other words, if I may break these statements down: (1) the capitalist mode of production emerges as a historically specific phenomenon; (2) through its power, it homogenizes society, thereby enabling the derivation of general laws (which an emphasis on historical particularity precludes); (3) by compelling other societies into the capitalist mode of production, it universalizes these laws; (4) the temporality of the capitalist mode of production becomes the criterion for inclusion in history, and all pasts or modes of production not incorporated into this temporality are rendered into remnants of the past, or are marginalized; and (5) the whole process is endowed with a positive value, as is evident in the rhetoric of civilized versus barbarian, national one-sidedness or local narrow-mindedness against world consciousness, the idiocy of rural life, or the sentimentality of family life.

Marx and Engels, of course, wrote the *Communist Manifesto* to proclaim the imminent demise of the bourgeoisie at the hands of the proletariat. The *Manifesto* is also replete with references to the barbarism of the bourgeoisie and even to the deterioration of life under the capitalist mode of production for the great majority of the people. Where non-European peoples are concerned, Marx and Engels clearly believed that they do not welcome capitalism with open arms but, on the contrary, are compelled into it under the threat of extinction.

The point here is not that Marx was an apologist for capitalism but that his critique of capitalism (and expectation of its demise) presupposed the spatial and temporal restructuring of the globe by capitalism. This presumption made the spatiality and tempo-rality of the capitalist mode of production into the structuring principle of historical materialism. At the most obvious level, the proletariat, the very class to establish socialism, was a product of the capitalist mode of production, which meant that, spatially and temporally, socialism presupposed the teleology of capitalism. Capitalism, however, played a second, and equally important, part in the liberation of humankind; it liberated humanity from its own illusions, even if the price paid for such liberation was a profound dissolution of society and the beliefs that held society together: "All that is solid melts into air, all that is holy is profaned, and man is at last compelled to face with sober senses, his real conditions of life, and his relations with his kind." [14]

Where non-European societies are concerned, capitalism, as a prerequisite for liberation, has an implication that is not obvious within the European context. Whether or not Marx (or later Marxists) was Eurocentric by inclination, by turning a historical phenomenon into a universal prerequisite of liberation, histori-cal materialism in its very structure presupposed Eurocentrism. Although Marx drew a clear line between the capitalist mode of production and the pre-capitalist past in Europe, the latter was nevertheless the "womb" within which capitalism had assumed shape, and, as the "prehistory" of capitalism, it shared the his-torical claims of capitalism. For non-European societies, which had to confront capitalism as an external force, however, the his-torical claims of capitalism suggested that they had no history at all and, therefore, no subjective identity that they could bring into the world of capitalism. From this metahistorical perspective comes the meaning of the "Asiatic Mode of Production," which "explained" why Asians had no history while affirming the histori-calness of Europe. As the capitalist mode of production became universalized (if only by compulsion), Europe would bring history to Asia; in the process, to become historical, Asians would have to remake themselves in the image of the "bourgeoisie"—which, in Marx's time at least, could only mean the European bourgeoisie.

The teleology of capitalism, for non-Europeans, also meant inexorably the teleology of modern Europe, and for Marx, as much as for the European bourgeoisie, that was good.

What is interesting about Chinese Marxism is that it problematizes the spatial and temporal presuppositions imbedded in historical materialism. The basic issue in this discussion is the possibility of resistance to capitalism among non-European peoples, and whether such resistance implies alternative conceptualizations of time and space to that of the capitalist mode of production and, by extension, as I have argued above, within the theoretical structure of Marxism, that may help us think about the future in different ways. In skipping from Marx's writing in mid-nineteenth century to Chinese Marxism in the 1930s, I do not mean to imply that nothing of importance transpired during the intervening period in this regard. It has been argued that capitalism entered a new phase in the late nineteenth century (which I address again later), coinciding with full-blown colonialism, that in turn provoked anticolonial resistance movements all around the world. These resistance movements brought non-European peoples around the world into the struggle against capitalism, which within Marxist theory was to find expression in Lenin's reformulation of the problem of revolution (the direct source for Chinese Marxism). Theodor Shanin has argued that, towards the end of his life, Marx himself perceived in precapitalist social forms (in Russia, primarily) not just a source of resistance to capitalism but even possible models for future social organization.[15]

It is questionable, however, that these developments had a significant impact on the assumptions of spatiality and temporality that informed historical materialism. For Lenin, anticolonial resistance movements represented a "weak link" in the chain of global capitalism; the ultimate goal of breaking the link was not to bring about a political or economic re-fragmentation of the world, but to revive the possibility of revolution in Europe. If anything, the Communist International, established in 1919, sought to bring organizational unity (homogeneity?) to resistance movements and, therefore, to preempt such fragmentation. It is also difficult to argue, as Shanin does, that what Marx had to say on the *mir* in Russia had any significant impact on historical materialism as a way of thinking about the world. After all, Marxism retained its original spatial and temporal premises.

Chinese Marxism, too, would in the end uphold these same premises. I do not argue here that Chinese Marxism transformed the original Marxist assumptions about the world; on the contrary, such assumptions guide Chinese Communist policies to our day. The peculiarities of the Chinese revolution, however, forced into the open certain questions concerning Marxist spatiality and temporality, articulating basic problems in the conception of the world that they informed. It is these problems that I would like to sketch out here. I will return by way of conclusion to a discussion of why they may be significant in our day (as with Marx's own statements about the possibilities offered by the *mir* as social form).

Two aspects of Chinese Marxism are especially relevant here: Marxist historiography, or the rewriting of Chinese history from a Marxist perspective, and what I describe as "Chinese Marxism," a localized version of Marxism as universal theory that was articulated during the late thirties and the forties in the process of what Chinese Communists described as "making Marxism Chinese" (*Makesi zhuyide Zhongguohua*).[16] Both aspects were closely connected with problems that arose during the Chinese revolution, but, in spite of an ultimate coincidence in the direction they gave to Marxist theory in China, they were contradictory in certain fundamental ways.

Chinese Marxist historiography was (and is) quite complex in the relationship between theory, history, and politics that dynamized it and, therefore, in the conflicting conclusions it reached concerning China's past;[17] but it lends itself to generalizations on the questions of time and space that shaped its contours. Simply put, Chinese Marxists accepted the universality of Marxist formulations concerning European history and rewrote the history of China in a narrative that paralleled European historical development. The assumption in China that European historical categories could be universalized and thus employed in the rewriting of other histories did not begin with Marxist historians. The notion instead went back to the first modernist (and nationalist) rethinking of the past around the turn of the century. It became especially flagrant, though, with Marxist historians, who conjoined the assumptions of a universal history with the search for a Marxist orthodoxy.

Chinese Marxist historians, unlike Marx or European Marxists, were unwilling to deny China a history of its own. They therefore almost uniformly rejected the concept of an "Asiatic Mode of Production" (aided by the repudiation of the concept in Soviet historiography after 1930) and sought instead to bring the problematic of the Asiatic Mode of Production into a historical narrative conceived after a universal pattern that abolished significant differences between European and Chinese histories. In other words, they rephrased the problem of historical development to read: Why, having followed parallel tracks and being subject to the same laws of history, did Europe realize the fulfillment of history (in other words, capitalism) whereas China did not? The task of historical explanation was thus to identify those elements in Chinese society that had held back China's development. With the question posed in this manner, it is not surprising that, for most Marxist historians, it was those elements in Chinese society and culture that distinguished China's past from Europe's—the differences that spoke to China's identity—that accounted for China's inability to realize the promise of historical development and that represented, therefore, backwardness in Chinese society.

At the same time that they rejected the hegemonic implications of denying China a history, Chinese Marxists accepted, through their assertion of the universality of history that could be rendered plausible *only* by admitting that China had failed to realize the promise of that history, the hegemony of a Eurocentric temporality. This hegemony could hardly be disguised by treating the capitalist mode of production as a historical category that transcended any historically specific location. The abstraction, a product of the refraction of European historical development through the intermediation of theory, merely mystified its fundamentally Eurocentric spatiality and temporality. It simply enabled the application of the theory to Chinese history by obviating the need to ask embarrassing questions about the history imbedded in the theory itself (although, we may note here, Marxist historians were quite quick to charge interpretations that they disapproved of with imposing European schemes on China's past!). The consequences need not be belabored: Judged against this Eurocentric temporality, what was different in China's past appeared not just different and, therefore, pregnant with alternative historical possibilities, but backward and residual, a fetter on History.

What needs brief comment are the spatial implications of this assumption of a universal temporality that took the capitalist mode of production as the fulfillment of historical development. These are not to be explained as automatic products of the Marxist theoretical assumptions that guided the rewriting of Chinese history, for Marxism here also served to fulfill nationalist longings for the reconstruction of political space; nevertheless, Marxist theoretical concepts served these longings well. Whether we speak of space in a literal sense (such as a national political space, the space created by a national market, or relations between town and country, center and locality, or state and society) or in a metaphoric sense (such as the social spaces implied by concepts of family, class, gender, ethnicity, culture), judged against the homogenization of space that had informed Marx's own social teleology under capitalism, the diversity and fragmentation that had characterized pre-capitalist Chinese society appeared as the very emblems of the backwardness that had arrested China's historical development, rather than as possible social moments out of which an alternative spatiality could be constructed.

In either case, Marxist historiography, in its assumption of a universality patterned after a European narrative of historical development, also gave priority to the theory that articulated the dynamics of that narrative over the particularities of Chinese history. China's arrested development, then, could be reactivated only through the introduction into Chinese society of the dynamic forces of the capitalist mode of production, either with capitalist development *or* with a socialism whose task was to develop capitalism in order, ultimately, to transcend it. The rewriting of history after the Eurocentric teleology of capitalist modernity ruled out the possibility of looking into the past as a source of possible future alternatives to this teleology.

I would like to backtrack here for a moment and state what Chinese Marxist historiography *did* so that we may better appreciate what it did not do. This view of history was not just an exercise in futility. By bringing historical materialism, and Marxist theoretical concepts, into the analysis of China's past, Marxist historians achieved a virtual revolution in Chinese historiography. The new theory revealed problems about China's past to which previous historiography had been oblivious. Comparisons with European history (and other histories), however tendentious, nevertheless made possible unprecedented insights into the workings of Chinese society, into social relations, modes of production and exploitation, issues of class and gender, political relations, as well as into problems of thought and culture. Furthermore, Marxist historians examined in depth questions pertaining to China's development in a capitalist world, which was in a basic sense the point of departure for Marxist historiography. Their discussions were quite reminiscent of what since then have become worldwide discussions on the capitalist world system and its implications for non-EuroAmerican societies (the "Third World"). Not a few of them, while they still pointed to the deleterious effect of China's past on its present, nevertheless saw China's "underdevelopment" as a consequence of global capitalist development, and saw in "delinking" (to use Samir Amin's term) China from the capitalist world-system the only possible solution to the problems of China's development and national integration (which is not very surprising, given the Leninist inspiration in Chinese Marxism).

The issue, therefore, is not whether or not historical materialism played a crucial role in Chinese historiography as a source of critical insights, which it indubitably did. The more relevant points concern the limitation of the conclusions Marxist historians drew from what they discovered in China's past by their ready acceptance of the social and historical teleology of historical materialism, and their stereotyping of the social and cultural phenomena of the past with concepts that seemed to be immune to evidence of social diversity.

It was mainly in the latter regard, what we might describe as "the confrontation with the concrete" (in James Wilkinson's words),[18] that "Chinese Marxism" as it was formulated in the late thirties went beyond Marxist historiography by problematizing the spatial and temporal presuppositions of historical materialism—which is not very surprising. Marxist historians were for the most part revolutionary intellectuals, but intellectuals nevertheless. Although their writing of history was motivated by the need to resolve immediate questions of revolution, they were nevertheless somewhat removed from the demands of everyday revolutionary activity. "Chinese Marxism" was formulated during the course of revolutionary activity and represented the abstraction of direct revolutionary experience.

What I describe as "Chinese Marxism" here was a product of the Yan'an Period of Chinese communism (1935–1947), closely corresponding to the World War II years in China, and grew out of the experiences of the Communists with revolution in rural China, where they had been forced after 1927. The formulation of "Chinese Marxism" was the work of Mao Zedong and a group of Marxist intellectuals who served more or less as his advisors. The work was centered around what Mao in a speech in late 1938 described as "making Marxism Chinese" (or, as it is more conventionally called, "the sinification of Marxism"). I have described my understanding of "Chinese Marxism" elsewhere; here I will briefly sketch its main outline, since it bears on the present discussion.[19]

The Communists have consistently described "making Marxism Chinese" as "the application of the universal principles of Marxism to the concrete circumstances of Chinese Society," which I think says considerably less than what the formulators of "Chinese Marxism" had in mind. In 1938, when he first broached the idea, Mao Zedong invoked the long history and culture of China that, he insisted, must be part of any consideration of China's future. During the same years, Communist ideologues frequently referred to the need to bring a Chinese "sensibility" (*guoqing*) into Marxism. By the early 1940s, a close advisor of Mao, Ai Siqi, was proclaiming that the Chinese revolution, in its very practice, was itself expressive of the universal principles of Marxism.

"Chinese Marxism" is not, however, merely an application of Marxist theory to China's circumstances. It is best understood as a localized or vernacular version of a global Marxism that claimed a subject position for itself within a universalized Marxist discourse. Chinese society was not merely a target for the arrow of Marxist theory (as Mao put it on one occasion), but an active moment in the universalization of Marxism whose presence and characteristics must be acknowledged in any formulation of Marxism as universal, not just European, theory. If I may break down "Chinese Marxism" into its presuppositions, these would be: (1) Chinese Marxism was a universal Marxism; that is, it shared with all Marxisms certain basic principles; (2) Chinese Marxism was a Third World Marxism, a Marxism that was the product of circumstances that bore a different relationship to capitalism than either Europe or the Soviet Union (the Marxism, in other words, of a "semi-colonial semi-feudal society," as the formulation went); (3) within this Third World status, Chinese Marxism was also a national Marxism that must recognize China's historical and cultural characteristics; and (4) what rendered this Marxism truly vernacular was a recognition that Chinese society itself was composed of localized cultures that could not be contained within the conception of a uniform national cultural space. Forced on the Communists, above all by the exigencies of guerilla warfare, this recognition was expressed at the very fundamental level of language—that the Communists, in revolutionizing Chinese society, must accommodate and incorporate into their own theoretical language the various languages of the people at the local level. Just as they must transform the culture of the people in accordance with a Marxist vision, so must that vision be itself transformed by the people's input and their own cultural characteristics.

What occurred here was the fragmentation of the theoretical space of Marxism, as well as the recognition of the possibility that the future, to emerge from the reconstruction of these spaces, would not necessarily accord with the temporal assumptions of Marxism—not the immediate future anyway. "Chinese Marxism" presupposed, moreover, not only a fragmentation of space but also a contradictory relationship between these fragmented spaces; contradiction not just in the obvious sense of opposition but also of unity, which ultimately gave the various oppositions a coherent meaning. The contradictions that were the products not just of China's historical legacy but of capitalism (First World/Third World, global/national, national/local, local/local, etc.) also appeared as contradictions within the theoretical space of Marxism. These contradictions, moreover, did not lend themselves to resolutions that could be predicted from theory but must be worked out historically, which endowed the future with a good measure of uncertainty. It is not very surprising that the articulation of "Chinese Marxism" in the late 1930s coincided with the articulation of a Maoist version of Marxism to which the concept of contradiction was central. Mao, we may remember, also posited that contradictions would persist into the foreseeable future, into socialist and even into communist societies, which ruled out the possibility of defining ahead of time what such societies might look like. Only death, he observed philosophically, puts an end to contradictions.

The fragmentation of global space into so many spaces of differing scope was accompanied in "Chinese Marxism" with a proliferation of the categories of theoretical analysis. Such categories were further broken down into *their* localized manifestations, a fragmentation that nearly threatened to do away with categories and theoretical abstractions and, therefore, with theory itself. Conceptual fragmentation, too, had to do with the exigencies of guerilla struggle, although there is evidence that it preceded the guerilla phase of the Chinese revolution and was rooted in a political conception of Marxism (against an economic one) that introduced a political calculus into the problem of revolution (a similar, though cruder, breakdown of categories is visible in some of Lenin's writings, especially writings on agrarian society). In agrarian society in particular, the Communists quickly had to recognize that social conflict could not be reduced to conflict around class interests, but had to acknowledge conflicts informed by a multiplicity of social relationships, from gender and kinship relations to ethnic relations, with everything in between. Even the same category had to be broken down into its many manifestations, since there was no way of predicting political orientation and affinity from theoretical abstraction. Mao recognized this problem as early as 1926, and the concern this insight generated is revealed in the various rural investigations that the Communists undertook as part of the revolutionary struggle in the countryside. A category such as class, to take one example, was too crude for analyzing political orientation, for attitudes were shaped not just by class interests (which itself concealed hierarchies within the same class) but by the whole web of social relations that defined social and political location. The categories concealed, in other words, the fact that political and social orientations were "overdetermined" by the conjuncture of a multiplicity of social relations, of the past and the present, and of material circumstances and intangible cultural legacies. Here, too, spatial fragmentation (in both a literal and a metaphorical sense) and temporal uncertainty (the uncertainty created by conjunctural circumstances) called for historicizing theory in the "confrontation with the concrete."[20]

These characteristics of "Chinese Marxism," as I have outlined them here, are responsible for the image of a "populist" or more democratic socialism that Mao's Marxism for some time conveyed to the outside world, as well as to many people in China (including non-Communists), that distinguished Mao from Stalin, or even from Lenin and Marx.[21] And there are no doubt genuine differences, if only because of different spatial and historical locations. On the other hand, it is erroneous, I think, to assume that the qualification of theory in "Chinese Marxism," or the various assertions of a "Chinese style socialism," "socialism with Chinese characteristics," and so on, added up to the recognition of social and historical possibilities other than those embodied in a Marxist spatiality and temporality and, by extension, in the capitalist mode of production.

"Chinese Marxism," while it confronted the concrete in the course of revolution, remained wedded to the same social and historical teleology that informed Marxist historiography in China. China must still achieve the productive base that in the First World had been created by capitalism and in the Soviet Union by the Bolsheviks, because the Communists continued to view this productive base (the technology of capitalism) as the irreducible condition for socialism. Under the guise of revolution, while Mao ruled ("grasp revolution, promote production," was the slogan) and, more explicitly, in the post-Mao years ("use capitalism to develop socialism"), Chinese Communists have remained wedded to a productivist conception of socialism. The purpose of social transformation was to serve the cause of development (which over and over again took priority over the social goals of revolution), a development informed by its roots in the capitalist mode of production. Similar treatment occurred with the categories of theoretical analysis. Though the exigencies of revolution forced a recognition of the complexity of theoretical categories and their disjuncture with concrete social phenomena, the categories in Chinese Communist thinking nevertheless continued to carry a teleological power; if they do not exist in social actuality, in other words, they must be made to exist, since open-ended categories render the future open-ended, which did not accord with the spatial and

temporal demands of the theory which retained its historical teleology. It should not be overlooked that the existence of a party
organization, which had assumed for itself the destiny of history,
endowed the teleology of theory with inescapably concrete political power. "Chinese Marxism" would in the end turn its back on
the revelations of the revolutionary struggle that had produced it.

To lay the entire Chinese experience at the door of Marxist
theory, as is often done these days, would be to overlook the roles
played by Chinese nationalism and by the global context. I have
stressed the role theory played in the outcome of the Chinese revolution because I am concerned primarily with the problematics of
Marxism here, and also because Marxist theory, as a theory of liberation, must take responsibility for its historical outcomes, even
where it is employed in the articulation of political outcomes not
of its own making (not solely of its making, anyway). But since
Marxism, like any other theory or ideology, does not exist in a
vacuum, it must be viewed in its historical context. In the case of
China, nationalism was to play a significant part in at least one
important respect. Chinese nationalism, while it obviously sought
the fragmentation of global space into various national spaces,
was much less tolerant when it came to the fragmentation of internal spaces, to any recognition that the vernacular should be
authentically local and not merely national. In the end, it was
not just Marxism that rendered local social and cultural varia-
tion recessive but, in addition, Chinese nationalism. Secondly, the
problem of nationalism itself, like the problems of Marxist theory
in China, must be viewed within the global context of imperialism. These days, when Chinese themselves feel secure enough in
their independence to afford forgetting what imperialism meant
to a previous generation, not many wish to speak about the ways
in which imperialism as a threat shaped the course of Chinese
nationalism, as well as of Chinese Marxism, and precluded serious
consideration of possible alternatives to EuroAmerican and Soviet
examples of development. The memory is important, nevertheless,

to a historical evaluation of Marxism, although it should not be allowed to conceal the responsibilities of theory for its historical outcomes.

It is to this broader historical context, to the changing relationship between capitalism and Marxism as it appears in historical hindsight, that I would like to turn now to consider how these abandoned alternatives of the past may have something to contribute to thinking about Marxism in our day.

Flexible Production

Are My Hands Clean?

I wear garments touched by hands from all over the
　　world
35% cotton, 65% polyester, the journey begins in
　　Central America
In the cotton fields of El Salvador
In a province soaked in blood, pesticide-sprayed
　　workers toil in a broiling sun
Pulling cotton for two dollars a day

Then we move on up to another rung—Cargill
A top forty trading conglomerate, takes the
　　cotton thru to the Panama Canal
Up the Eastern seaboard, coming to the U.S. of
　　A. for the first time

In South Carolina
At the Burlington mills
Joins a shipment of polyester filament courtesy of the
　　New Jersey petro-chemical mills of Dupont

Dupont strands of filament begin in the South
　　American country of Venezuela
Where oil riggers bring up oil from the earth for six
　　dollars a day
Then Exxon, largest oil company in the world
Upgrades the product in the country of Trinidad and
　　Tobago
Then back into the Caribbean and Atlantic Seas
To the factories of Dupont
On the way to the Burlington mills

In South Carolina
To meet the cotton from the blood-soaked fields of
　　El Salvadore

In South Carolina
Burlington factories hum with the business of
     weaving oil and cotton into miles of fabric
     for Sears
Who takes this bounty back into the Caribbean Sea
Headed for Haiti this time
May she be one day soon free

Far from the Port-au-Prince palace
Third world women toil doing piece work to Sears
     specifications
For three dollars a day my sisters make my blouse
It leaves the third world for the last time
Coming back into the sea to be sealed in plastic
     for me
This third world sister
And I go to the Sears department store where I buy
my
blouse
On sale for 20% discount

Are my hands clean? *

*Sung by Sweet
Honey in the Rock,
lyrics by Bernice J.
Reagon, based on
article by John Cava-
nagh, "The Journey of
the Blouse: A Global
Assembly." Quoted
from Cynthia Enloe,
*Bananas, Beaches and
Bases: Making Feminist
Sense of International
Politics* (Berkeley:
University of Cali-
fornia Press, 1990),
p. 158.

3

Socialism and Capitalism in History

Marxism historically has internalized the narrative of capitalism as its informing principle, as I have already argued. I would like to go further here and suggest that the demise of socialist states reveals another important aspect of the historical relationship between Marxism and the capitalist mode of production. So long as Marxists could convincingly claim the future for their visions of socialism and communism, it could be sustained that capitalism was one phase in a historical narrative whose end was communism; capitalism was the last phase of what Marx once described as "prehistory," following which humanity would realize authentic history. The fall of socialist states compels the conclusion that the reverse has indeed been the case: that the political history of Marxism has been part of the narrative of capitalism, in two senses. First, the historical transformations of Marxism, both politically and theoretically, have been bound up with changes in the nature of the capitalist mode of production. This is not to say that Marxism, and the political movements and resistance to capitalism that it inspired, were merely passive objects of history; on the contrary, it is arguable that such resistance played an important part in forcing and giving direction to changes within capitalism itself. Nevertheless, when all has been said and done, capitalism has proven to be the more dynamic force in shaping the course of history, and socialist societies as we have known them appear now to have corresponded to one phase within the history of capitalism. Second, and for the same reason, it is no longer possible to sustain convincingly that Marxism as we have known it in any serious sense points to a future that may transcend the capitalist mode of production.

Neither capitalism nor Marxism has remained static over the last century and a half. Without going into the troublesome question of the boundaries of a mode of production, and of how much or what kind of change is necessary before one mode of production turns into another, suffice it to say here that, even though the capitalist mode of production persists, it has gone through phases that differ significantly from one another in social and political organization, and even in the organization of production. Marxism, too, has changed significantly in response. The present seems to be another period of transformation in capitalism. Correspondingly, there is also a change occurring in ways of thinking about the world, represented in the proliferation of a variety of post-modernisms. These new world views have raised fundamental questions about the spatial and temporal assumptions of the narrative of capitalism and, therefore, of Marxism. Changes in the contemporary world appear to be so drastic that they have raised questions about whether or not past ways of thinking about the world (Marxist or otherwise) are relevant at all in the present; Wallerstein, for instance, has called for the "unthinking" (not merely rethinking) of social science.[22] Spatial and temporal considerations (TimeSpace) are crucial to Wallerstein's call, as they are to most post-modernist thinking (without implying here that Wallerstein considers himself post-modernist). I would like to examine these changes briefly, in further consideration of contemporary Marxism.

Political economists usually periodize industrial capitalism into three phases: (1) from the late eighteenth to the late nineteenth century, marked by the emergence of light industries, market economies, and the initial spread of capitalism outside of Europe; (2) from the late nineteenth century through World War II, corresponding to the emergence of heavy industries, the corporate organization of production, states as regulators of the economy and managers of social conflict, and, where the rest of the world was concerned, colonialism; and, (3) a post–World War II phase corresponding to the communications revolution, the transnationalization of production, the appearance of the transnational corporation as the locus of economic activity, and the change in the function of the nation-state from manager of internal conflict to manager of the global economy. Ernest Mandel calls this last phase "late capitalism"; others have named it "flexible production," "Global Capitalism," and so on, pointing to the unprecedented mobility under the new economic "regime" not just of commodities and financial transactions but of the very process of production itself.[23]

It is probably not fortuitous that the emergence of socialism as an alternative to capitalism and the political establishment of socialist societies coincided with the second phase of capitalism, while the phase of flexible production has brought about their demise. Socialist societies as we have known them have shared certain fundamental characteristics with the second phase of capitalism, may even be said to have been shaped by those characteristics. Economically, the concentration of production was common to both; the concentration of production around the turn of the century even suggested to Lenin that the economic basis for socialism had already been created by capitalist development. Second, state management of the economy and society was taken for granted both in socialist societies and in capitalist societies during this period. Finally, the assumption that the character of social relations would be dictated by the division of society into two major classes, as had been predicted by Marx, was also a common belief in both cases. In capitalist societies, from the late nineteenth century on, fear of social polarization into two conflicting classes was an important element in the advocacy of state intervention in society. In socialist societies, the ideological assumption that the proletariat must replace the bourgeoisie historically was to lead to a relentless commitment to homogenization by wiping out the bourgeoisie and converting everyone into the proletariat.

"Delinking" from the capitalist world system, which has been a major concern of actually existing socialisms, seemed quite feasible at a time when the capitalist economies themselves seemed to be taking the form of highly organized national economies with monopolistic corporations at their core. Socialism, it turned out, contrary to Marx, emerged not out of capitalist societies but outside of them, from the peripheries of the capitalist world economy in opposition to the capitalist core. Nevertheless, it bore upon it the stamp of its context within the new phase of capitalism.

The parallel drawn here between socialism and capitalism in its second phase obviously does not suggest identity between capitalism and socialism; only that socialism as political reality differed significantly from what Marx had had in mind. It was nevertheless an expression of a Marxism that had been transformed in response to changes within capitalism. E. H. Carr has observed that, while the Marxism of Marx was an expression (as critique) of the market economy phase of capitalism, Leninism represented the Marxism of the period of monopoly capitalism.[24] We may add that Leninism was also viewed as the Marxism of that phase of capitalism when, through the agency of monopolistic multinational corporations, capitalism became multinational as well, which meant that the resistance of peripheral societies became as important as, if not more important than, the struggle of the proletariat against the bourgeoisie. The fact that socialist societies originated in this phase of capitalism left its mark on the continual configuration of these societies; the reason socialist economies have seemed so out of date in recent years may be that, while capitalism after World War II was able to transform itself, socialist societies in their basic economic assumptions remained bound to this earlier phase.

Although the political reality was contrary to Marx's expectations of socialism, socialist societies remained committed to the basic assumptions of the Marxist narrative of development. These assumptions were now incorporated into the political ideology of the socialist states, which, if anything, even further reified the developmentalism of capitalism and committed socialism to strive for what had been achieved in Europe and the United States by capitalism. The ruthlessness of the state in exploiting society to achieve its developmental goals matched the ruthlessness of the most rapacious capitalist. Spatial homogenization became a measure of progress, compounded in its oppressiveness by the bureaucratic regulation of society. The bureaucratic state, identifying with its own administrative vision the abstract teleology of history, became even less tolerant of possible alternatives to its reified utopia than the bourgeoisie it repudiated.

However we may evaluate the achievements of socialist societies, it is undeniable that they were successful in one respect: establishing a productive base through ruthless measures of accumulation. (This ruthlessness seems overwhelmingly oppressive since it was through state power that accumulation was achieved and in the name of a socialism that was to benefit the people; but whether or not it was any more ruthless than initial capitalist accumulation, in spite of the fact that the latter was spread over a much longer span of history, is a historical question seldom asked and one that awaits serious inquiry.) But, the state-managed economies of socialist states differed from their counterparts in capitalist societies in two important respects (that is, two respects aside from obvious organizational differences between market and centrally planned economies). First, the second phase of capitalism had emerged out of an earlier, market economy-based phase that endowed capitalist societies with a far broader infrastructure economically and socially, giving them a flexibility that could not be matched in socialist societies which, in a way, had reversed the process of capitalist development. Second, even during their second phase when the nation-state took hold of the economy, capitalist economies remained multinational and global, which gave them a different dynamic than that of socialist economies that were never completely autarkic but turned inwards, nevertheless. It is quite clear in hindsight that socialist economies, committed to control and stability over dynamic growth, were ill-suited to realizing their own ideological commitments of matching, and surpassing, capitalist economic growth.

As long as the global economy was organized around national spaces, this stagnation, barely concealed, could be justified on the grounds of national defense and economic protection. The transnationalization of production, with the global economy it created and the seeming vitality of that economy, exposed socialist economies—and marginalized them. To the extent that socialist economies, to realize the development they promoted ideologically, opened their borders to the global economy, on the other hand, they were quickly destabilized by the transformative dynamics of capitalism. The basic problem of actually existing socialism was that it sought to mimic the economic achievements of capitalism, goals that not only distorted socialism but, because capitalism is obviously much better equipped than socialism to achieve capitalist goals, undermined the legitimacy of the system as well.

Much has been made of the stagnation of socialist economies as an explanation of the fall of socialist systems. Stagnation is itself a relative concept, and to assume that a society must fall simply because it does not register annual advances of one kind or another is to adopt tacitly the ideological premises of change and progress that are characteristic of the capitalist mode of production. Just as the emergence of socialist systems was tied with changes in capitalism, their fall, too, I think, requires attention to their context in the capitalist world economy. Not only had socialist societies from the beginning mimicked capitalism, but, more importantly, over the last three decades they entered increasingly intensive economic relations with capitalist economies in trade, finances, and scientific and technological exchanges that forced them into playing a game the rules of which had been set elsewhere—within the capitalist organization of the world economy. If I may for a moment set aside the question of whether or not national economic autarky is socially or politically desirable, it is worth noting that socialists, from Marxists in China in the 1920s to contemporary world system theorists such as Samir Amin and Immanuel Wallerstein, have long argued that "delinking" from the capitalist world system is crucial to autonomous national economic development.[25] We might even add that an attempt to achieve autonomous development is *all* that socialism has been, which is not very surprising since the conceptualization of socialism in all existing socialist societies is traceable to Lenin's analyses of imperialism and national liberation.

The point here is that the stagnation of socialist societies only became noticeable and unacceptable through contrast with the dynamism of global capitalism. The contrast underlined the vacuity of claims that socialism could do a better job than capitalism in achieving capitalist goals. But the question was more complex than just the relationship between socialism and capitalism. Socialism historically became indistinguishable from nationalism in these societies and was converted into an instrument of nationalist aspirations to power. This identification exacerbated the problem, for it precluded an independent socialist critique of the concern with national economic progress and, as the national economy lagged behind other national economies, increasingly turned socialism into an object of nationalist frustration as the culprit for economic stagnation. It was not very helpful, either, that Communist parties in these societies came to identify socialism with party power and resisted any efforts to formulate alternative conceptualizations of socialism.

The problem was not just ideological. Given an organizational basis that had been designed largely to meet the needs of an autarkic economy, intensifying economic relations with capitalist economies gave rise to what Marie Lavigne has described for Eastern Europe as a "disorganising effect."[26] Their organizational structure stood in the way of complete integration into the capitalist world economy, even as it became increasingly more incoherent while functioning on the peripheries of the world system. Socialism thus undercut the ability to formulate coherent policies internally. There was stagnation, in other words, but a stagnation that is best understood within the context of the economies' relationships to the capitalist world economy. Likewise, this same involvement with the world economy, however incomplete, produced social interests and orientations to which such stagnation was intolerable. I am referring here not just to the greater awareness of the differences between socialist and capitalist societies in styles of life, freedom, consumption, and so on (that inevitably accentuated the positive aspects of capitalist societies) that accompanied increased contact, but, more importantly, to the formation of social groups (from diplomats to professionals to groups that came to have economic ties to the world economy) with direct interests in the abolition of autarky in favor of integration with the capitalist world economy. It is ironic, though not surprising, that the initiative for such integration should have come from members of the ruling elite in socialist societies, including members of the Communist parties, who may well have wondered how much being a ruling elite was worth as long as the system prevented them from enjoying the benefits that seemed widely available in capitalist societies. So far, they would seem to be the only ones benefiting from the collapse of the systems over which they once presided!

Viewed from a world system perspective, finally, it appears that even more crucial in underlining the stagnation of socialist economies than the contrast with capitalist societies of the First World was the emergence of the Third World. By the late seventies, Lavigne observes, Soviet policymakers no longer considered the Third World "a homogeneous whole destined sooner or later to opt for the socialist path to development."[27] The director of the Institute of World Socialist Systems in Moscow wrote in 1980 that "it would be inaccurate to state that relations between the socialist world and the developing countries are built on the principle of socialist solidarity. No. We deal with states, the majority of which have chosen the capitalist path to development. Only a few of them have opted for socialist orientation."[28] This sense of marginalization was exacerbated by the emergence in the eighties of the Newly Industrializing Countries in the former "less developed" world. These countries not only demonstrated the efficacy of national integration with the capitalist world economy but outstripped socialist societies technologically and in the expansion of their export economies. They began to capture global markets for commodities that socialist policymakers had hoped to provide.[29] As the Third World seemingly surged forward, in other words, the former "Second World" seemed to be slipping back into "Third World" status, not just in economic and technological performance but in increasing foreign debt and financial dependence. Most significantly, socialist countries experienced a bifurcation in their national economies, into a weak export sector, barely able to compete within global markets, and into an internal sector, barely, if at all, connected with the export sector. As Lavigne put it shortly before the collapse of socialism in Eastern Europe:

> A world socialist economy cannot stand as an alternative to a world capitalist economy. In consequence, the standard UN three-term division into developed market economies, developing market economies and centrally planned economies is hardly relevant any more. . . . East-South relations, wrongly considered in the West as duplicating the pattern of North-South relations, are increasingly "South-South" relations of a specific type. This in turn points to East-West relations as a South-North pattern, where the socialist countries of Europe feature as inefficient NIEs (Newly Industrializing Economies).[30]

When leaders of the capitalist world speak of the victory of capitalism (or often, more euphemistically, democracy) over socialism, they imply that this victory was a planned victory, for which there is some evidence. Although it is not clear what the plan might have been (except perhaps creation of export economies through the World Bank and other similar institutions to facilitate global economic ties through the agency of transnational corporations), there is some evidence of conscious manipulation of the global economy in order to tie the Third World closer to the First. The plan may have been to undercut the possibility of socialist revolutions there and, therefore, to marginalize socialist states both economically and politically and force *them* into the capitalist world economy. In 1980, greeting Ronald Reagan's presidential victory, editor of *Time* magazine (and Trilateralist) Hugh Sidey, wrote:

> For quite a while now the bright young men of the State Department have seen the potential of the multinational free marketplace. They have urged that the U.S., the godfather of this commercial era, do all it could to nurture multinational corporations, to bring in the Third World and its resources and even to entice Communist countries to take part. The idea was simple: get a number of nations interlocked in retrieving raw materials, manufacturing goods and distributing products, and the people who do this work and prosper from it will form a powerful influence within each country fighting against any disruption of the system by political elements [or, in the case of "communist countries," we presume, a group fighting to disrupt the existing system].[31]

A policy of attracting revolutionary or socialist states within the orbit of capitalism rather than containing them militarily represented a shift from the foreign policy strategy that had prevailed in the United States in the immediate aftermath of World War II. When and where this new orientation emerged is not clear; it was visible in the Trilateral Commission's conceptualization of the world when it was founded in 1963 and probably received a boost from the debacle in Vietnam, which showed the futility of attempts to suppress Third World revolutions by force.[32] Its goals were finally accomplished in the eighties under the Reagan-Thatcher leadership of the capitalist world.

It would be misleading, however, to focus too much on conscious manipulation and conspiracy and to ignore the systemic conditions of this victory: the emergence of a Global Capitalism in the years after World War II. This development, too, it is arguable, may have been the product of policy; but its realization required as its prerequisites new technologies that would make possible the globalization of capitalism, which has also changed the nature of the capitalist mode of production. If there is any validity to what I have argued above, that the incorporation of the Third World into the capitalist world economy was also responsible for transforming the relationships between socialist and capitalist societies, this new global economy must be the point of departure for any consideration of the fate of socialist states, as well as the future of capitalism. The capitalist world economy to which socialist states returned in the seventies and eighties was a significantly different capitalist world economy than at the time of Karl Marx or, more to the point, at the time of Lenin, whose analyses had given direction to the course of actually existing socialisms. This new world economy must, therefore, provide the point of departure in considering the future of Marxism as well.

Fundamental to the structure of the new Global Capitalism is what Froebel and others have described as "a new international division of labor": in other words, the transnationalization of production where, through subcontracting, the process of production (of the same commodity even) is globalized.[33] The novelty of this process has been questioned by, among others, Wallerstein, who has observed that "commodity chains" ("integrated production processes") have been characteristic of capitalist production from its origins.[34] Be that as it may, new technologies have expanded the spatial extension of production, as well as its speed, to an unprecedented degree. These same technologies have also endowed capital and production with unprecedented mobility, so that the location of production seems to be in a constant state of change, seeking maximum advantage for capital against labor, as well as to avoid social and political interference (hence, "flexible production"). For these reasons, most analysts perceive in Global Capitalism a qualitative difference from similar practices earlier. The organizational and cultural consequences of the new division of labor attest to these qualitative differences.

Second is the "decentering" of capitalism nationally. In other words, it is increasingly difficult to point to any nation or region as the center of Global Capitalism. More than one analyst (I am referring to analysts in positions of power) has found an analogue to the emerging organization of production in the northern European "Hanseatic League" of the early modern period (one of them describing it as a "high-tech Hanseatic League"). In other words, the system consists of a network of urban formations, without a clearly definable center, whose links to one another are far stronger than their relationships to their immediate hinterlands.[35]

The medium linking this network, third, is the transnational corporation, which has taken over from national markets as the locus of economic activity. This entity is not just a passive medium for the transmission of capital, commodities, and production but determines the nature of the transmission and its direction. Although the analogy with the Hanseatic League and the appearance of production suggest decentralization, production is actually heavily concentrated behind the facade of these corporations. One articulate spokesman for the new economic order suggests that the share of decision-making for production between the corporation and the market is roughly 70 to 30 per cent.[36] With power lodged in transnational corporations, which by definition transcend nations in organization and/or loyalty, the power of the nation-state to regulate the economy internally is constricted, while global regulation (and defense) of the economic order emerges as a major task. This state of affairs is manifested not only in the proliferation of global organizations but also in efforts to organize extra-national regional organizations to give coherence to the functioning of the economy.

Fourth, the transnationalization of production is the source at once of unprecedented unity globally, and of unprecedented fragmentation (within the history of capitalism). The homogenization of the globe economically, socially, and culturally is such that Marx's comments about capitalism cited previously, premature for his time, finally seem to be on the point of vindication. At the same time, however, there is a parallel process of fragmentation at work, globally, in the absence of a center to capitalism and, locally, in the fragmentation of the production process into subnational regions and localities. Supranational regional organizations such as the European Economic Community, Pacific Basin Economic Community, and the North American Free Trade Zone (to mention some that are the objects of intense organizational activity) manifest this fragmentation at the global level, and localities within the same nation, competing with one another to place themselves in the pathways of transnational capital, represent it at the most basic local level. The formation of nations themselves, it is arguable, represented attempts historically to contain fragmentation, but under attack from the outside (transnational organization) and the inside (subnational economic regions and localities), it is not quite clear how this new fragmentation is to be contained.[37]

Another important (perhaps the most important) consequence of the transnationalization of capital may be that, for the first time in the history of capitalism, the capitalist mode of production appears as an authentically global abstraction, divorced from its historically specific origins in Europe. In other words, the narrative of capitalism is no longer a narrative of the history of Europe. For the first time, non-European capitalist societies are making their own claims on the history of capitalism. Corresponding to economic and political fragmentation, in other words, is cultural fragmentation or, to put it in its positive guise, "multi-culturalism." The most dramatic instance of this new cultural development may be the effort over the last decade to appropriate capitalism for the so-called Confucian values of East Asian societies, a reversal of a long-standing conviction (in Europe and Asia) that Confucianism was historically an obstacle to capitalism. I think it is arguable (as I will argue here) that the apparent end of Eurocentrism is an illusion. Capitalist culture, as it has taken shape, holds Eurocentrism in the very structure of its narrative, which may explain why, even as Europe and the United States lose their domination of the capitalist world economy, culturally European and American values are still dominant globally. It is also noteworthy that what makes something like the East Asian Confucian revival plausible is not its offer of alternative values to those of EuroAmerican origin but its articulation of native culture into a capitalist narrative. Having said this, it is important to reiterate nevertheless that the question of world culture has become much more complex than in earlier phases of capitalism.

The fragmentation of space, and its consequences for Eurocentrism, also imply a fragmentation of the temporality of capitalism: The challenge to Eurocentrism, in other words, is that it is now possible to conceive of the future in ways other than those common to EuroAmerican models. Here, once again, it is difficult to distinguish reality from illusion, but the complexity is undeniable.

Finally, the transnationalization of production calls into question earlier divisions of First, Second, and Third Worlds. The Second World, the world of socialism, is, for all practical purposes, of the past. But the new global configuration also calls into question the distinctions between the First and the Third Worlds. Parts of the earlier Third World are today on the pathways of transnational capital and belong in the "developed" sector of the world economy. Likewise, parts of the First World, marginalized in the new global economy, are hardly distinguishable in way of life from what used to be viewed as Third World characteristics. It may not be accidental that the north-south distinction has gradually taken over from the earlier division of the globe into three worlds; although we must remember that the references of north and south are not merely to concrete geographic locations but are metaphorical references: north denoting the pathways of transnational capital and, south, the marginalized populations of the world, regardless of their location.

These features of Global Capitalism, and the very concept itself, are subject to some qualification. Global Capitalism (or flexible production) is still capitalism. This new formation of capitalism is new only in the sense that it represents new solutions to old problems: how to maximize profits, how to establish controls over markets in the face of competition, and how to liberate production and markets from social intervention (such as labor struggles) and political controls (such as state intervention). Whether or not flexible production as an answer to these problems is effective, or will be effective in the long run, is highly debatable. The new problems generated by flexible production have not replaced but rather added to older problems. Even the new solutions themselves are not entirely new but recall earlier configurations of capital, as with the "Hanseatic League" as a paradigm for comprehending the motions of capital at the present.

The concepts of Global Capitalism or flexible production are actual descriptions of contemporary realities and, at the same time, imaginary constructs regarding capital. As descriptions, they impart a sense of new modes of production, organization, and marketing. They are also creative inventions, however, because what they describe is an economic, social, political, and cultural formation that is highly unstable and contradictory in its operations. As such, they represent a discourse that presents an ideal (or wishful thinking) about capital—what yet remains to be achieved —as if it were already a reality of the world, disguising the many contradictions that drive capitalism as it is. The globalization of capital renders the discourse persuasive since now, in contrast to the past, capital has a global constituency. But the same globalization recreates older contradictions in new forms.

This contradiction may be most evident in the relationship between global capital and nations as economic or political entities. I observed above that the new Global Capitalism erodes the power of nations and transforms the function of the nation-state. Transnational corporations, in their organization as well as their activities in production and consumption, have created a transnational class of professionals and managers, dependent groups that are tied to it through subcontracting and other mechanisms, global patterns of consumption, and, with it, a global culture. At the same time, however, competition over and control of markets are still the concerns that dynamize capital and, in this competition, transnational corporations still freely call on the ideology of nationalism to achieve their goals. However transnational their operations and their ideologies, when in difficulty the corporations readily reassert their "Americanness," "Japaneseness," or "Chineseness." It is probably not accidental that globalism finds its most enthusiastic advocates among the more powerful transnational corporations with bases in the economically stronger states (the Trilateral or Triad areas of the United States, Western Europe, and Japan). Newcomers on the scene (such as corporations from Taiwan and South Korea) are more visibly tied to the nationality and nation-states of their origins. Even in stronger states, the smaller/weaker corporations or those that find themselves in trouble (such as Chrysler) readily play the nation card. That flexible production characterizes a new phase of capital should not disguise the persistence of these serious contradictions. Stated somewhat differently, awareness of the persistence of such contradictions (which I discuss in more detail later) is crucial to thoroughly understanding Global Capitalism or flexible production as critical concepts, against the purposes of ideological hegemony that they may serve in the discourse of transnational capital.

More than any other socialist state, the case of China illustrates the implications for socialism of the new configuration of global capitalism, mostly *because* it was more successful than others in adjusting to capitalism *and* has so far survived the collapse of other socialist states. The incorporation of China into Global Capitalism after 1978 created the same "disorganizing effects" as it did in other socialist states, culminating in the profound crisis of 1989. The socialist state survived that crisis by ruthlessly suppressing the opposition and reaffirming its commitment to socialism. But what kind of socialism has survived, and how long can it last?

Since the immediate issue here is not socialism as an abstraction but the historical relationship between socialism and capitalism, I will answer the first question bluntly by saying that contemporary Chinese socialism, the so-called "socialism with Chinese characteristics," is the socialism of the period of flexible production. Its main features are: (1) "A planned market economy," which simply means introducing market mechanisms into a centrally planned economy to alleviate the inefficiencies of the latter. It has its antecedents in the "market socialism" that emerged earlier in Eastern Europe. The introduction of the market internally, however, must be viewed within the broader context of an incorporation of the national market into a Global Capitalism, which means that there is much more to the adoption of the market than the abandonment of a strictly central planned economy; it also represents the abandonment of a socialism conceived in terms of national economic autarky. (2) Therefore, whereas in an earlier period Chinese socialism (following the Soviet example) mimicked First-World capitalist development in its second phase (with emphasis on building a national productive base), in this new context it mimics the Newly Industrialized Countries (NICs), of which the most successful examples are found, it so happens, on China's immediate geographical boundaries. Economic development is conceived, therefore, as the development of an export-oriented economy. Subcontracting, which played a major part in the development of the NICs, already has tied the Chinese to the global economy.[38] China also seeks to attract foreign investments by giving privileges to foreign companies; not incidentally, the special economic zones that played an important strategic part in the development of the NICs have also been utilized by China to this end. The special economic zones are significant because they create spaces for the activities of transnational corporations, while retaining the fiction of national economic sovereignty (and control). In Chinese development strategy, the importance assigned to special economic zones reached its zenith in 1987, when then premier Zhao Ziyang suggested that all of coastal China be converted into a special economic zone. (3) This mode of development would seem to be creating an economic configuration based around regional nodes: Guangdong (and Hainan) in the south in connection with Hong Kong; east China (Shanghai to Fujian) increasingly in connection with Taiwan; northeast China, in connection with Japan, South Korea, and, possibly, the eastern provinces of Russia. This internal regionalization of the national economy is accompanied externally by efforts to incorporate the Chinese economy into supranational regional economic entities; the choices expressed here (reflecting global uncertainties about regional formations) have ranged from the Pacific Basin Economic Council to an East and Southeast Asian economic region to a "greater China" economic region encompassing China, Taiwan, Hong Kong, and Singapore (although the latter has been downplayed recently because of its evident, and disturbing, chauvinistic implications).[39] (4) As with other states in the present period, as the initiative for economic development shifts downwards and the state gradually abandons its role as the guarantor of public welfare, its coercive functions as the guarantor of national stability and unity comes to the foreground. In China, as elsewhere, the nation in an economic sense (a national market or a national planned economy) has become meaningless under the forces of transnationalization, on the one hand, and internal regionalization, on the other hand. The nation-state still serves an important function, however, in guaranteeing spaces for the free flows of capital and commodities and, conversely, standing guard against the economic forces of fragmentation. (5) The new situation is expressed at the ideological level in the idea of "using capitalism to develop socialism." This jingle, however, conceals a more fundamental change: an effort to integrate socialism and capitalism, which, concretely, translates into the creation of a national economy that has been incorporated into a global capitalist economy under the supervision of the Communist Party that, more nakedly than ever before, identifies socialism with its own power and economic interests.[40] Economic and social fragmentation has, however, found expression at the ideological level, evidenced by the total disintegration of ideological unity. China may be a society that is still "modernizing" economically and technologically, but ideologically it is already "post-modern," for every idea from the most contemporary to the most reactionary seems to find a constituency. For the same reason, different ideas of the future are in contention, pointing to a fragmentation of time that corresponds to the ongoing fragmentation of space.

The question under these circumstances is not whether or not socialism can last, or for how long, but rather whether or not socialism has any meaning in contemporary China. The fall of Eastern European socialist states, who invented the concept of "market socialism," has demonstrated already that "market socialism" is a socialism without a future. Even more significant, I would suggest, is the incorporation of socialist economies into a global capitalism of flexible production with its dynamics of fragmentation, which renders irrelevant the national organization of the economy that has been a premise of socialism as we have known it. In spite of the suppression of the opposition in 1989 and reaffirmations of socialism, 1989 did not make much difference in China as far as these dynamics are concerned. The so-called conservatives in China dismissed Zhao Ziyang, with his grandiose ideas about a coastal special economic zone, but the conversion of coastal areas into special economic zones continued without interruption nevertheless.[41] The recent national congress has once again reaffirmed the commitment to using "capitalist methods to develop socialism." The ultimate question, therefore, becomes one about the ability of the Communist Party to convert itself successfully into an overseer of an economy that is fast becoming part of Global Capitalism. The very success of the Chinese Communist leadership so far in incorporating China into the capitalist world economy, in much more eloquent fashion than the fall of socialisms in Eastern Europe, traces for us the trajectory of socialism's history within the larger narrative of the capitalist mode of production.

The Culture
of Modernity

Paul Ricoeur writes:

The phenomenon of universalization, while being an advancement of mankind, at the same time constitutes a sort of subtle destruction, not only of traditional cultures, which might not be an irreparable wrong, but also what I shall call for the time being the creative nucleus of great cultures, that nucleus on the basis of which we interpret life, what I shall call in advance the ethical and mythical nucleus of mankind. The conflict springs up from there. We have the feeling that this single world civilization at the same time exerts a sort of attrition or wearing away at the expense of the cultural resources which have made the great civilizations of the past. This threat is expressed, among other disturbing effects, by the spreading before our eyes of a mediocre civilization which is the absurd counterpart of what I was just calling elementary culture. Everywhere throughout the world, one finds the same bad movie, the same slot machines, the same plastic or aluminum atrocities, the same twisting of language by propaganda, etc. It seems as if mankind, by approaching *en masse* a basic consumer culture, were also stopped *en masse* at a subcultural level. Thus we come to the crucial problem confronting nations just rising from underdevelopment. In order to get on to the road toward modernization, is it necessary to jettison the old cultural past which has been the *raison d'etre* of a nation?*

Cogent statement of an old problem! But it does not go far enough. Where do "nations" and "underdevelopment" come from? And what of the "creative nuclei" of not-so-great cultures, the "folk societies" of Robert Redfield, who might be able to hold before great civilizations and nations, whose core values have also legitimized hierarchy and oppression, images of what Barrington Moore, Jr., has described as "the decent society?" *

*Paul Ricoeur, *History and Truth* (Evanston: Northwestern University Press, 1965), pp. 276–77.
*Robert Redfield, *The Little Community: Peasant Society and Culture* (Chicago: The University of Chicago Press, 1965); Barrington Moore, Jr., "The Society Nobody Wants: A Look Beyond Marxism and Liberalism," in *The Critical Spirit: Essays in Honor of Herbert Marcuse*, ed. by Kurt H. Wolff and Barrington Moore, Jr. (Boston: Beacon Press, 1968), pp. 401–8.

4

Marxism in the Age of Flexible Production

Let me recapitulate briefly the historical relationship between Marxism and capitalism as I have outlined it: (1) A first phase, corresponding to the nineteenth century, when Marx posited the incorporation of the entire globe into a capitalist world economy. He viewed this process as a devastating but progressive development since it dynamized societies that for centuries had been slumbering. "World-space," to Marx, was the space created by an expanding European capitalist economy that homogenized societies it brought within its compass; just as "world-time" was the temporality of European capitalism. Socialism, which would be ushered in by the overthrow of the bourgeoisie by the proletariat (the European proletariat, for all intents and purposes), presupposed the universalization of capitalism. (2) A second phase ran from the late nineteenth century through World War II. During this phase capitalism indeed became global, but, instead of homogenizing the globe as Marx had thought, it led to new kinds of divisions for two reasons. First, the globalization of capitalism intensified national competition in the core areas of Europe and North America (as well as in Japan) while simultaneously spreading nationalism across the globe, which called forth resistance to the homogenizing dynamics of capital. Second, the expansion of capitalism from the European core made possible the further development of capitalism in the core areas, but instead of universal development, its consequence in the peripheral areas was to create underdevelopment (that is, to render peripheral economies into appendages of the capitalist core). Crucial to Lenin's reformulation of Marxism was a recognition that the struggle for national political and cultural autonomy in peripheral societies must also take the form of resistance to underdevelopment. National liberation, in other words, entailed not just political and cultural liberation from European domination but also liberation from the hegemony of capital. Given the economic inequality between the core and the periphery, such liberation must take the form of "delinking" the national economy from the capitalist world economy in pursuit of autonomous development.

The expansion of capitalism did not homogenize the world but, rather, created two new worlds of development and underdevelopment. As the continued development of capitalism and political reform deradicalized the socialist movement in core areas, revolutionary socialism against capitalist domination shifted to the periphery, where it became merged with the struggle for national liberation. The emergence of the first socialist state in Russia after 1917 further divided the world into the "three worlds" of social theory, which was to gain currency after World War II (remembering, as we must, that the Second World of socialism emerged later historically than the world of underdevelopment that came to be described as the "Third World"). The struggle of this period, which sharpened in the years after World War II, was a struggle between capitalism and socialism over the hearts and minds of the people of the Third World.

It is important to underline here that this division of the world did not stop ideological homogenization. Political, cultural, and economic resistance to EuroAmerican capitalism during this period was very real, and an effort was made in Third World nationalisms (as in the case of China) to bring a national cultural voice into considerations of space and time. At the same time, however, nations of the Second and Third Worlds alike assimilated the spatial and temporal assumptions of capitalism that were built into the very notion of development (in its bourgeois modernizationist *and* socialist versions alike). Socialism itself, a source of revolutionary nationalism, also appeared as an instrument of national development. The contradiction between parochial national concerns and an expansive capitalism in the core states was paralleled in socialist and Third World states by a contradiction between parochial national concerns and the social and global aspirations of socialism; with the end result that nationalist developmentalism in the name of socialism exploited and oppressed the very laboring groups that were the constituencies of socialism.

(3) A third phase, which gained recognition increasingly from the seventies on, was launched when the globalization of capitalism assumed a configuration that seemed to confirm Marx's predictions of the midnineteenth century, although retaining the core-periphery configuration (and the corresponding development-underdevelopment situation) albeit in a new form. Capitalism has indeed become universal, based not only on the globalization of commodity exchange and financial transactions but, most importantly, on the transnationalization of production through a "new international division of labor." It is possible, as Wallerstein and others have argued, that the transnationalization of production is nothing new, since "commodity chains" have characterized the capitalist economy from its origins, which may be the reason that some analysts seek to comprehend the new configuration of capitalism through analogies with the early period of capitalism's history, such as the Hanseatic League. These analogies, carried too far, however, may be reductionist, for the differences between the new phase and earlier ones are quite significant. Whereas earlier capitalist development led to the emergence of Europe as the core of a capitalist world economy, the contemporary transnationalization of capitalism, by creating nodes of capitalist development around the globe, has decentered capitalism, put an end to Euro-American economic domination of the world, and has abstracted capitalism for the first time from its Eurocentrism. Whereas earlier capitalist development, in the midst of global homogenization,

resulted in the formation of national economic units (or at the least, was conjoined to the development of national economies), in the new phase the globalization of capital tears down national boundaries, undermines national economic sovereignty, and abstracts capitalism from the nation as the unit of development. The most significant unit of the new global economy is the transnational corporation. Though there are aspects to the transnational corporation that are reminiscent of the great companies of early capitalist development (such as the East India Company), contemporary transnational companies pride themselves on being authentically transnational, without significant roots in the national soils from which they sprang. Unlike the mercantile goals of earlier companies, which represented a collaboration between state and economic enterprise, the new transnational corporations represent the liberation of capital from state and society, so that their activities corrode the power of the nation-state as well. A condition, as well as a result, of the domination of transnationalism in the world economy is the emergence of a global professional-managerial class, and even a global culture.

Spokesmen for the new economic configuration of the world have described it as a "global regionalism" or a "global localism,"[42] which captures the simultaneous homogenization and fragmentation at work in the world economy. Production and economic activity (hence, economic "development") become localized in regions below the nation, while its management requires supranational supervision and coordination. In other words, the new pathways for the development of capital cut across national boundaries and intrude on national economic sovereignty, which renders irrelevant the notion of a national market or a national economic unit, and undermines national sovereignty from within by fragmenting the national economy. Similarly, the necessity of supranational coordination transforms the functions of the nation-state from without, incorporating it within larger regional or global units. Those areas of the world that are on the pathways of capital (or manage to place themselves on those pathways) develop and become more alike than ever before socially, culturally, and politically; the rest has to fend for itself the best it can in a state of intensified economic, political, and cultural marginalization.

The transnationalization of capitalism also has done away with the division of the world into three worlds; for as regions in the Third World have emerged as centers of activity for capital, regions in the First World have been marginalized into Third World status. The core-periphery relationship, in other words, has become abstracted from the nation, becoming a characteristic of global relationships between capital and those marginalized by capital as well as of intranational relationships between different regions; hence, the irony in the contemporary world of simultaneous cosmopolitanism and localism. This new development, just as it has undermined the nation-state in capitalist societies, has also corroded socialist states that were premised historically on national economic sovereignty. With the fall of socialist states, the world has reverted into a twofold division once again between a First World of transnational capital and a Third World of underdevelopment, with the formerly second socialist world reduced to "Third World" status, trying to climb out of that status by placing itself in the pathways of capital. The two-way division of the world into north-south (which, not surprisingly, emerged as concepts accompanying this new situation) describes the current phase of capitalism more accurately, as long as we remember that they refer not to geographical location but to location in the configuration of the world economy: north meaning on the pathways of capital, south, outside of them.

Socialism as we have known it, based as it was on premises of national autarky and delinking from the capitalist world economy, is irrelevant under the new circumstances. So is Marxism as the ideology of socialist states, and even Marxism as a theory of global modernization. To the extent that Marxism as theory is informed by the spatial and temporal assumptions of a Eurocentric capitalism, it has no way of accounting for the new situation of capitalism, which is characterized as much by fragmentation as it is by homogenization. Capitalism itself has sought to transcend its origins by recognizing this fragmentation. It may be no surprise that the initiative for efforts to comprehend the world economy in new terms has come from without EuroAmerican capital.

It does not follow, however, as some have claimed, that the new world situation represents the victory of modernization over Marxism or revolution, or that the modernization theory that was formulated in the aftermath of World War II in competition with Leninist strategies is better able than Marxism to account for the developments in the world economy.[43] Indeed, it is arguable that Marxism failed only where it overlapped with modernization theory, and that Marxism as ideology revealed its own contradictions most sharply when socialism took it upon itself to achieve the productionist goals of capitalism.

The reasons that modernization theory is insufficient to account for the new developments in the capitalist world economy are not very obscure. In spite of the important qualifications introduced into modernization theory by those such as Samuel Huntington, who were quick to recognize the vulnerability of the economism of modernization theory to the socialist political challenge, modernization theory to this day retains in its structure the spatial and temporal teleology of capitalism; if anything, more deterministically than Marxism. Now that socialism has disappeared as a competitor, this teleology has once again come to the forefront, perhaps most insistently in the former socialist societies: that the development of production will lead automatically to the political, social, and cultural characteristics of modernity, including general welfare. "Socialist" modernizers, or what is left of them, as in China, simply continue to insist that modernity will also result from socialism. Symptoms to the contrary, regardless of how serious and insistent they may be, are consequently attributed to the "backward" legacy of the past that must be cleared away for modernization to succeed. We may add, however, that to account for the partial move to modernity of societies that refused to abandon their pasts and out of an honest effort to disassociate modernization from Eurocentrism, there has on occasion also been an effort to discover modernity in non-European pasts. The latter, obviously, does not much affect the teleology of modernization, because it simply brings non-European pasts into the axis of modernization. What modernization theory has done consistently is to suppress its origins in capitalism by representing itself as an abstraction, a theory of development without spatial and temporal boundaries. This contention even made it possible for a while to recognize Marxism as an alternative theory of modernization—which was correct, in my view, but for the wrong reason. What rendered Marxism legitimate from the perspective of modernization theory points exactly to what have been its failures as a radical critique of capitalism.

Given this teleology, modernization theory is no better equipped than a modernizationist Marxism to account for the contemporary world. If anything, the refusal of modernization theory to address the problem of spatial relations within capitalism has more often than not rendered it into a barely concealed apologetic for the teleology of a Eurocentric capitalism. By spatial relations, I am referring here to relations within the same society between different groups which occupy different locations in the social relations of capitalist production, to relations between nations, which are as much the units of analysis in modernization theory as they are in Leninist Marxism, and, finally, to relations between global core-periphery formations that emerge from the relationship between development and underdevelopment. Ignoring these relationships has also implied ignoring unequal power as a determinant of such relationships as well as obviating the necessity of grasping resistance to capitalism not simply as an expression of past legacies but as a very product of the relationships themselves. Modernization theory has turned a blind eye to the fact that such resistance could be, and was, overcome only through political and economic coercion. Hence the ideology of modernization has drawn its power from wishful thinking (as ideological as anything else) that sooner or later all will join the march of progress, following the models of more advanced groups, nations, and societies. The theory has thus attached itself to the progress of capitalism through time and simply ignored those left out of such progress, or postponed their inclusion in the march of progress to a later time.

Where the failure of this ideology is most evident in our day is in the economic and social regression of formerly "advanced" societies, such as the United States, which gives the lie to assumptions of ceaseless progress. Just as such regression jumbles up the temporality of a bygone day, the intermixture of First and Third Worlds across national boundaries similarly confounds the spatial teleology of a capitalism progressively developing nations, regions, and the whole globe. Indeed, those in responsible positions within the world economy readily concede that recent developments within capitalism have benefited only a small portion of the world's population within and across nations, with the great majority (the "south") reduced to a position of marginality and increasing immiserization.[44] In the midst of global unity and homogenization, moreover, there are unmistakable signs of fragmentation within nations and globally, which more than anything else undermines the modernizationist teleology and accounts for the increased consciousness of time and space in contemporary culture.

This new consciousness has expressed itself in a variety of "post-modernisms." Fredric Jameson has described "post-modernism" as the "cultural logic of late capitalism."[45] Similarly, in his recent book, *The Condition of Post-Modernity*, David Harvey has drawn direct parallels between post-modernism as a way of thinking and "the regime of flexible production or accumulation."[46] Crucial to the understanding of contemporary culture in either case is the fragmentation of time and space; the distinctive feature of post-modernism, according to Jean-Francois Lyotard, is "incredulity toward meta-narratives."[47] Modernization as a "metanarrative" is today no more relevant than a Marxism that shares in the spatial and temporal metanarrative of an earlier capitalism—or socialism.

Indeed, Marxism as theory has been much better able than modernization theory to account for the spatial relations of capitalism. For all his assumption of spatial homogenization under capitalism, Marx based his analysis of capitalist society on antagonistic social relations, which introduced a notion of social space into his analysis. Lenin, by recognizing the importance of the relationship between nations and regions and between development and underdevelopment, grasped capitalism in its full spatiality. The importance of space was most explicitly and fully grasped in "world system" analysis, which, while not bound by Marxism in a strict sense, nevertheless is an outgrowth of Marxist analysis of the world. Unlike Lenin, moreover, who was concerned primarily with capitalist relations under imperialism, world system analysis in the hands of Wallerstein and Fernand Braudel has been employed to explain the whole history (and even the prehistory) of the capitalist mode of production.[48]

Given the importance of spatial relationships in the current phase of capitalism, world system analysis is of crucial relevance in accounting for the present-day configuration of the capitalist world economy. It seems to me, however, that, to meet this task, Marxist theory must disassociate itself from two other teleologies: the teleology of the temporality of capitalism, and its own conceptual teleology, the expectation, in other words, that concepts of analysis (such as class) must of necessity be realized in concrete social existence. In light of the discussion above, it is also clear that nations no longer serve as useful units of analysis (in the motions of capital), which world system analysis has grasped from the beginning, perhaps too fervently in downgrading the importance of politics independently of economic structures.

In his recent, *Unthinking Social Science*, Wallerstein has disavowed not only a Eurocentric temporality but called into question the notion of development itself, including development as it has been incorporated into a unidirectional Marxist utopianism.[49] What merits some attention here is the conceptual teleology of Marxism, central to which is the idea of class. The concept of class may be more crucial to social analysis today than ever before (recall the previous statements about contemporary United States politics), but over the last few decades class analysis has been complicated vastly by competing social concepts that must be incorporated into any critical analysis. The obvious ones are gender, ethnicity, and race, which appear in almost all critical writing these days with the regularity of established cliches. Equally important is a body of work from E. P. Thompson's *The Making of the English Working Class* to James Scott's recent work, which has demonstrated the ways in which class, used as a rigid category, has served to disguise rather than explain social actuality. Rather than a hermeneutic tool of social analysis—class being one category among others in a web of social relations that is not reducible to any one of its moments—class has been rendered into a determinant of the totality of social existence.[50] The political implications of this tendency are shown to be equally horrendous: In existing socialist societies, the abstract notion of class was appropriated by the vanguard leadership, to be used to deny the complex social existence of the laboring classes themselves, to remake them forcefully to meet the image of the abstraction. This kind of teleology has not only proven to be politically and socially dangerous, it is hardly appropriate at a time when the structure of social existence and individual consciousness appears more blatantly than ever as the overdetermined product of complex social relationships.

The resemblance between these points and those I made when discussing the practice of Marxism in the Chinese revolution in the 1930s (and, by extension, comparable situations in other Third World revolutions) is not accidental. I noted previously that, by committing itself to the temporal teleology of Marxism (and its embodiment in the Communist Party), Chinese Marxism turned its back on what its own practice had revealed concerning the relationships between Marxism and Chinese society, socialist and nationalist goals, concepts and social existence. Without claiming a premature post-modernism for Chinese Marxism, I would like to suggest here that there may be some parallels between the political flexibility called forth by a guerilla revolution and the flexible production of contemporary capitalism. Chinese Marxism (dare I say the Marxism of Mao), disassociated from the teleology of the Communist Party, thus becomes an appropriate Marxist paradigm for an analysis of the contemporary world.

It may not be fortuitous that, though Chinese and other radicals around the world have repudiated Mao's Marxism for its consequences in China, the language of this Marxism lives on in the conceptualization of the world by the managers of Global Capitalism. Thus, one advocate of "guerilla marketing" says:

> 1984 is here, the problem is how to manage it. The answer we propose, gentlemen, is guerrilla marketing. Just as the guerrilla fighter must know the terrain of the struggle in order to control it, so it is with the multinational corporation of today. Our terrain is the world. Our ends can be accomplished with the extension of techniques already in the process of development. The world market is now being computer micromapped into consumer zones according to residual cultural factors (i.e. idioms, local traditions, religious affiliations, political ideologies, folk mores, traditional sexual roles, etc.), dominant cultural factors (i.e. typologies of life-styles based on consumption patterns: television ratings, musical tastes, fashions, motion picture and concert attendance, home video rentals, magazine subscriptions, home computer software selection, shopping mall participation, etc.), and emergent cultural factors (i.e. interactive and participatory video, mobile micromalls equipped with holography and super conductivity, computer interfacing with consumers, robotic services, etc.). The emergent marketing terrain which must be our primary concern can only be covered totally if the 304 geographical consumption zones already computer mapped (the horizontal) can be cross referenced not only with the relatively homogenous "conscious" needs of the macroconsumer units, but also with the heterogenous multiplicity of "unconscious" needs of

the microconsumer (the vertical). This latter mapping process has so far readily yielded to computer solution through the identification and classification of a maximum of 507 microconsumption types per macroconsumption unit. Through an extension of this mapping, even the most autonomous and unconventional desires may be reconstructed for the benefit of market extension and control. Emergent marketing strategies must move further beyond the commodity itself and toward the commodity as image, following marketing contingencies all the way down. And here, precisely, is the task of guerrilla marketing: to go all the way with the images we create and strike where there is indecision flowing from constructed situations without determinant outcomes just like the guerrilla fighter. For the multinational of today profits are necessary but not sufficient conditions for growth which our whole history shows to be equivalent to survival. We remain dependent on market control and extension. But now this requires more than the control of production and consumption—to grow we must sell a total image. Like guerrilla fighters, we must win hearts and minds. This task can be accomplished by constructing and reconstructing them all the way down in what can only be viewed as an endless process.[51]

Cleansed of its computer vocabulary, this text would read very much like one of those local analyses upon which the Communists based their guerilla strategy in the 1930s.[52] But the resemblance does not stop there. As with guerilla struggle where the requirements of a fluid strategy called forth a need for organizational flexibility in order to deal with diverse circumstances without abandoning long-term organizational goals, the imperatives of guerrilla marketing, too, have resulted in a reconceptualization of the transnational corporation as an organization. "Global localism" implies, organizationally, that the corporation domesticate itself in various localities without forgetting its global aims and organization. The contradictory roles companies must fill have created organizational problems that resemble closely those of a centralized Communist Party engaged in guerilla warfare. The CEO of one such company, who chooses to describe his company as "multi-domestic" rather than multi- or transnational, describes the organizational problems his company faces much as Mao used to describe problems facing the Communist Party of China: "ABB [Asea Brown Boveri] is an organization with three internal contradictions. We want to be global and local, big and small, radically decentralized with centralized reports and control. If we resolve those contradictions, we create real organizational advantage."[53]

The radical slogan of an earlier day, "think globally, act locally," has been assimilated by transnational corporations with far greater success than by any revolutionary strategy. As with the Communist Party of China in politics, however, the recognition of the local in marketing strategy does not mean any serious acknowledgment of the autonomy of the local but is intended only to incorporate localities into the imperatives of the global. The "domestication" of the corporation into local society serves only to mystify further the location of power, which rests not in the locality but in the global headquarters of the company, which coordinates the activities of its local branches. As the Japanese marketing analyst, Kenichi Ohmae, put it on one occasion (again, sounding much like Mao), "global localism" is "seventy percent global and thirty percent local."[54] The guiding vision of the contemporary transnational corporation is to homogenize the world under its guidance. The same CEO writes: "Are we above governments? No. We answer to governments. We obey the laws in every country in which we operate, and we don't make the laws. However, we do change relations *between* countries. We function as a lubricant for worldwide economic integration [emphasis in the original]."[55]

Some lubricant, that which "changes" the relations it facilitates! It points to a crucial point, nevertheless: that transnational corporations of today, much like radical guerillas, do not just respond to circumstances but create the conditions for their success. To achieve this end, however, they must first grasp social, political, and cultural relations in their full complexity rather than rely on abstract categories of analysis. The categories appear in their analyses, as they did in Mao's writings, for example, as hermeneutic tools rather than as descriptions of social reality. The goal of analysis itself is not to fulfill social need but to formulate the teleology of the organization, although that teleology must be articulated with local languages to acquire legitimacy transnationally.

If the managers of Global Capitalism sound like Maoists, it is not, needless to say, because they are Marxists or Maoists but rather because they face a situation that parallels that of guerilla revolutionaries, who also seek to articulate theory with concrete local circumstances. Their task, in other words, is to domesticate the capitalist mode of production in diverse localities without compromising the global imperatives of capital. Their analyses represent attempts to account for (and to contain) contradictions that are the very products of the globalization of capitalism. Two elements seem to be of special significance in generating these contradictions. The first has its roots in local resistances to capital, which acquired prominent visibility in the second phase of the capitalist mode of production. Local resistance ranged in form from the assertion of national economic autonomy against capitalist hegemony to the literally local, where precapitalist social relations persisted in resistance (or, at the least, as obstacles) to relations of production and habits of consumption conducive to the penetration of capital. The reaffirmation (we might even say, conscious invention and articulation) of native culture and habits has been part of this resistance and integral to its language. Capital has responded by appropriating this language as its own, if only, as the statement on guerilla marketing clarifies, to disorganize local cultures and habits so that they may be "reconstructed" in accordance with the imperatives of capitalist production and consumption. The price, however, has been (if only on an interim basis) the fragmentation of the language of capital itself.

This problem was a product of earlier phases of capitalism, as it expanded from Europe and North America, when it was unambiguously Eurocentric and local cultural resistance carried a certain plausibility in targeting EuroAmerican domination of the world. What makes the contemporary situation genuinely contemporary is the successful globalization of capital, which points, on the one hand, to the successful breaking down of earlier resistances and, on the other hand, to the "deterritorialization" of capital from its EuroAmerican roots.[56] Ironically, the very success of capital has given rise to a new set of contradictions. The emergence of non-EuroAmerican capitalisms has been accompanied by the emergence of new voices that challenge EuroAmerican models by calling for forms of organization that are derived from alternative cultural constructions. The most recent instance is the notion of a "communitarian capitalism" as opposed to "individualistic capitalism." Although "communitarian capitalism" may be a mystifying oxymoron, and resorting to a native cultural legacy may be only a reconstruction of the past in response to the demands of capitalism, the issue, nevertheless, is the conflict over hegemony with global capitalism.[57]

The same globalization of capital has given rise to an unprecedented competition for markets in new areas of the world, which has intensified attention to local consumption habits, even if this is at bottom a competition over who can best "reconstruct" local consumption habits. Instead of concentrating on abstract research and development to determine the nature of a product, which could be sustained under conditions of monopoly, companies now have to take into account concrete habits of consumption and concrete circumstances of marketing. The prime example of this new reality is the automobile industry where, as Japanese producers never tire of saying, United States producers lost markets because they were oblivious to consumer circumstances. Finally, globally and locally, the success of capitalism has also meant the diversification of the constituencies of capital both as producers and as consumers, which means that capital now has to account for social groups that were earlier of marginal interest at best: women, ethnic groups, age groups, and so on. These social groups, too, must be disorganized to be "reconstructed," which means that they may no longer be perceived in terms of abstract categories but must be analyzed in their full overdetermined complexity and consciousness.

The goal, at any rate, is to fragment social existence and consciousness in order to reconstruct society globally, following the vision of a global capitalism. Under contemporary circumstances, however, fragmentation is as much a condition of social existence as homogeneity. In structural terms, we could describe these circumstances as products of a "conjuncture of structures," the structure of global capital with the structure of local existence; in the computer language that is so dear to managers of capital, it is an "interface" situation. Literal spatialization as well as the spatialization of categories are thus very much a condition of existence; and so is uncertainty about temporality, because a conjuncture, overdetermined as it is, does not permit easy predictions of the future. A global vision and transnational organization may help contain the contradictions (as the Communist Party of China sought to contain them with Marxist theory and party organization), but since the vision and the organization must be adjusted to account for the contradictions, for the time being the contradictions are a prime object of concern.

Marxism as ideology is dead. Marxism as theory is hardly irrelevant, much less dead. Stripped of its teleology, Marxist theory lives on in corporate analyses of the world, on the one hand, and in the many post-modernisms of contemporary radical criticism, on the other hand. But this is a Marxism that has been fragmented, its coherence as theory undermined, and its concepts deconstructed. It is a Marxism that appears in the form of contradictions and is open, as such, to conflicting appropriations. Capital has assimilated it for purposes quite different from the original intentions of the theory. Against the "real-world" power of capital, radical criticism seems to be able only to parody the fragmentation that it criticizes because, unlike the former, which may hope still to "reconstruct" contradictions with the teleology of the capitalist mode of production, post-modern criticism which has rightly abandoned all teleology has neither a guiding vision nor, in the face of what the organizational history of Marxism has revealed, the will to argue for any organized activity.

Where does this leave Marxism as theory and a discourse of

liberation? It is ironic (or maybe not ironic at all) that Marxism should fall out of favor, viewed with suspicion even by formerly Marxist radicals, at the very moment when the realities of capitalist society appear closest to Marx's predictions in the *Communist Manifesto* a century and a half ago, when capital has liberated itself from territorial restrictions to become truly global, when classes appear more genuinely transnational than at any time in the history of capitalism, and when the homogenizing effects of capitalism are more visible than ever before in the reproduction/replication of the same social and cultural formations globally. Few radicals bother to ask these days whether the fall of socialist states is an indication of the irrelevance of Marxism, or if it provides an excuse for those whose class interests—whether in capitalist or formerly socialist societies—demand that Marxism as a political discourse be discredited and "buried" (in Margaret Thatcher's vindictive terminology) forever.

The relevancy of Marxism is especially pertinent for two aspects of Marxism as a discourse: its insistence on totality, and the primacy it gives to class analysis. Post-structuralist repudiation of totality is echoed routinely in contemporary radical discourse in the repudiation of all "foundational" historical discourses, including those discourses that recognize in capitalism a "foundational" status in modern history, which also fetishizes "fragmentation" and "difference" as the source of democratic solutions to problems of inequality and oppression.[58] The concept of class, similarly, has come under criticism for "privileging" one particular form of oppression (and the struggle against it) over others, for insisting on the possibility of "fixed" social positions, and for its assumption of a subjectivity that is fixed by class location. The two issues are, upon close analysis, hinged together; the primacy of class as social category rests upon the foundational status of capitalism, and to deny primacy to class oppression and struggle immediately invites questions about the foundational status of capitalism in society and history.

It should be clear from what I have said above, which I will elaborate further below, that I view totalizing solutions of the kind associated with actually existing socialism as neither possible or desirable. It is quite another matter, however, to assert that any analysis of contemporary problems (and possible solutions to those problems) can dispense with the notion of totality under capitalism or with the problem of class as an issue of the first order. The repudiation of totality obviates the necessity of confronting a fundamental contradiction that faces contemporary radicalism: how to formulate non-totalizing solutions out of a situation where the forces of control and oppression are quite totalistic in their reach and implications. Indeed, avoiding this fundamental question may be responsible for blurring the distinction in so much radical criticism at the present between criticism and legitimation of prevailing forms of social disintegration and oppression, so that radical criticism often sounds like an ideological articulation of the capitalist system. Radicals ironically yield the impression of complicity in the system of oppression that they claim to be criticizing. This is especially evident in the repudiation of class (which is quite different from its qualification, of which more later). A morbid preoccupation with the "death of the subject" or ceaseless assertion of the complexity and contradictoriness of subject positions, however sound they may seem in tautological abstractions, ignores that in everyday life some people push the buttons and others, by far the great majority, have their buttons pushed without ever knowing why or how. Such arguments fail to acknowledge that some non-subjects command the wealth of the world while others starve. The denial of the "subject" in criticisms of ideology pulls the rug out from under the feet of resistance and the struggle against oppression and exploitation. Politics rendered into "identity politics" only ends up negating politics in any significant or meaningful sense.

In the introduction to this essay, I suggested that the concept of class, in its very abstractness, enables confrontation with the abstract operations of power under capitalism (and actually existing socialism). Needless to say, the concept of class, like any other

concept, is vulnerable to a teleological and/or reductionist interpretation, which renders it into a reified social category stripped
of its complexity in everyday life and opens it up to ideological
and political manipulation. The very abstractness of class identity,
however, makes it difficult (if not, in the long run, impossible) to
foreclose the intrusion of other demands on political identity, and
allows continued resistance to the reduction of political space to
the space of classes. Competing concepts such as gender, ethnicity,
etc., however crucial to radical analysis in pointing to alternative
constructions of social and political power, in their very concrete
associations invite identification readily, and easily disguise behind a facade of concrete unity the power relations (such as the
class interests of their purveyors) that animate them; hence they
are rendered into instruments of ideological manipulation, which
at the extreme leads to an exclusivist (and, in the case of ethnicity, vicious) biological politics—which characterizes so much
of politics globally at the present.

It seems ironic (and self-defeating) that the notion of "totality"
should be repudiated when so much of the theoretical activity at
present is devoted to overcoming the conceptual reductionism of
past theoretical approaches in criticism. The urge to reveal social
categories in their interrelatedness (or, as I prefer, overdeterminedness) already presupposes a space that is larger than that provided
by any one category. What is at issue, this suggests, is not the
notion of totality, but rather how we spatialize totality (where to
draw its boundaries, in other words) and whether or not "totalizing" of necessity requires reductionism (totalizing in terms of
one or another category). "The politics of difference" demands
cognizance of and respect for differences between social groups
and close attention to the autonomy of the local as opposed to
the homogenizing implications of totalizing. In neither case does
the assertion of "difference" make sense without reference to a
larger totality: in the case of social groups, without reference to
other social groups, and, in the case of the local, without reference to the extra-local, however defined. However much we may

sympathize with the programmatic assertion of "difference," the implied suggestion here of autonomy with regard to either social groups or localities is almost naive in its voluntarism and is self-contradictory.[59] It seems designed, above all, to avoid confronting the problem of capitalism, which provides the broadest context for any notion of social (as distinct from ecological) totality and the location for the theoretical discourse itself. Just as social existence is overdetermined by the web of social relationships that, ultimately, are themselves configured by this context, it is counter-productive and epistemologically misleading to assert the priority of the local over the global as if the local may be comprehended in isolation from the global. To do so is especially misleading under Global Capitalism, where the local emerges to the surface of consciousness as it is worked over by the intrusion and operations of capital.

It is difficult to see, at any rate, how any discourse of liberation can eschew confronting the problem of "totality," when that notion is essential to a comprehensive "cognitive mapping" of the circumstances of liberation, if not to its goals.[60] "The politics of difference" blurs the distinction between structure and homogenization; that the assertion of a structuring of the world by capital automatically implies a world homogenized by capital, which is obviously not the case, as structure itself implies difference in the relations that constitute it. The repudiation of "totality" in radical criticism only deprives radicals of the ability to "map out" the relations that constitute the world, leaving that task to the managers of Global Capital who do not share their qualms about totality. Indeed, in their obfuscation of the realities of global power, radicals provide an ideological cover for the operations of capital, confounding as the promise of liberation the problems it brings to the surface daily with these operations.

Why a sense of "totality" may be more important than ever under Global Capitalism may be illustrated through contemporary class formations. In his *Sociology of the Global System*, Leslie Sklair has suggested that the ascendancy of transnational capital has been accompanied by the emergence of a "transnational capitalist class," which works for transnational capital, facilitates its operations globally, and universalizes the culture and ideology of capitalism.[61] Ideologues of transnational capital not only confirm this phenomenon[62] but underline the ways in which it structures global relations, including the reconfiguration of relations between the First and the Third Worlds. Robert Reich, analyst of Global Capitalism and the current secretary of labor in the Clinton administration, is one important analyst (more important than before by virtue of his status) who seeks to adjust the United States economy to the new world situation created by Global Capital. According to Reich, the globalization of capital has transformed the nature of labor. He analyzes labor into three categories—"symbolic-analysts," routine production workers, and general service workers. Power, whether within the national economy or in the international division of labor, Reich argues, is based on the performance of "symbolic-analytical" functions that are crucial to the current phase of capitalism. Reich has little to say about that miniscule portion of the population that controls about 50 percent of the assets in the United States economy, but even so, the division of labor to which he points is instructive. Those who work with their minds (the "symbolic-analysts") constitute the ruling class within the national and the global economies, while those who work with their hands (routine production workers, formerly the "proletariat," and service workers) are the economic underclass (to say nothing of those marginalized by Global Capitalism). The division between mental and manual labor as a determinant of class position may not be new, but it is now global. It also characterizes the division of the world into First and Third Worlds, because command of symbolic-analytical functions (hence, research and development) points to power within the global economy while routine production and service work is relegated to the domain of the Third World. Class divisions in the global economy thus correspond to First and Third World (global as well as internal) divisions, both resting upon the division of labor between mental and manual labor.[63]

The point here is not about whether such analyses are beyond reproach in their representations of the world, which at this time of radical transformation may be a good deal more complex and unpredictable than these descriptions suggest. The point is that ideologues of Global Capitalism such as Reich (or the *Harvard Business Review*) analyze its operations with far greater clarity, in comprehensiveness and with attention to local ramifications, through once unspeakable (for the establishment) conceptualizations that putative radicals are anxious to repudiate; and for good reason, as they must iron out wrinkles in the global economy in order to consolidate it and secure the power relations it has produced. Failure of nerve or ideological innocence no doubt plays a part in the way radicals have avoided questions about totality and class thrown up by Global Capitalism. In some cases, as I will suggest later, however, the new-found power of "radicals" who themselves are products of circumstances created by Global Capitalism may have something to do with their avoidance of the problems of capitalism, which also obfuscate their own location within contemporary relations of power.

These considerations are important in answering the question I posed at the beginning of this book about Marxism's relevance in a contemporary strategy of resistance. I have argued above that the internalization in Marxism of the spatial and temporal assumptions of the capitalist mode of production has undercut the ability of Marxism to serve as a genuine basis for resistance to capitalism and even accounts for the hegemony of capitalist spatiality and temporality over Marxist formulations on liberation. The restoration of a Marxist teleology (the "latency of socialism within capitalism," in Fredric Jameson's words), therefore, offers no solution to the problems of Marxism. Neither does a conceptual teleology that confuses analytical categories with the overdetermined social existence of everyday life, or the reductionism of a class analysis which ignores the complex web of social relations that involve determinations other than the locus (and logos) of economic relationships. Past experience shows clearly that such teleologies do not produce democratic results politically because, as recent criticism rightly points out, they ignore difference and heterogeneity that must be factored into any agenda of liberation. Speaking theoretically, Marxist teleology no less than a bourgeois modernizationist teleology is incapable of dealing with the spatial and temporal fragmentation produced by Global Capitalism, which, if it is to be confronted in its concrete *structural* complexity, demands a complex and contradictory appreciation of totality that eschews spatial and temporal reductionism. The challenge, ultimately, is to evolve a non-totalizing discourse of liberation with a theoretical discourse that of necessity must address the problem of totality (however fragmented) under capitalism; which is another way of saying that the utopian goals of liberation must be separated out and rescued from the colonization of the future by the scientistic claims of theory.

The problem here, of course, is that a Marxist analysis stripped of spatial, temporal, and categorical teleology—in other words, a Marxism that has been rendered into one set of hermeneutic tools among others, to recall Ricouer—however appealing in its open-endedness, is also subject to appropriation for purposes quite contrary to the goals of liberation. I have noted above that Chinese Marxists in the thirties, having revealed through practice the *problematique* of teleology, turned their backs on what their practice had revealed by restoring the teleology of theory and organization—and for good reason. The assimilation of the language of guerilla socialism to Global Capitalism reveals the vulnerability of a Marxism turned into a social hermeneutic, where it can serve any master!

Problematic as such a conclusion is in stripping the future of certainty, it is still preferable to the despotism of scientistic theory.

Liberation is an ethical, rather than a theoretical, proposition, which implies that the goals of liberation must be formulated independently of theory and that theory must be placed in the service of liberation rather than the other way around, as has been the Marxist practice in the past. Resistance to homogenization and to the destructive developmentalism of the capitalist mode of production that dynamizes it must be the point of departure for liberation. The goals of liberation, however, cannot be defined theoretically, for theory itself presupposes homogeneity and the containment of diversity. Presently, there does not seem to be any viable resistance to the destructiveness or the hegemony of the capitalist mode of production and to the power of transnational corporations engaged in guerilla warfare against the great majority of humankind. What resistance does exist seems to be so fragmented that it offers no hope against the global coordination of capital. The lack of an organizational center to resistance or of a shared agenda in terms of which resistance movements replicate one another in the pursuit of a common goal, however, should not be taken as the absence of movement. Resistance movements are everywhere. That they are localistic and particularistic in the goals they pursue does not mean that they are unaware of the global forces at work that produce the particular problems they take up, or that they are incapable, therefore, of coordinating their activities in networks that transcend localities and particular interests. Primary examples are found in women's and ecological movements around the world. These movements are in the process of formulating agenda of liberation in the very process of their activities to resolve questions of everyday life, questions that are thrown up by the penetration of global capitalism into everyday life at every locality around the world. To subject them to abstractly defined agenda, as in the past, would add up only to preempting localized creativity in the pursuit of liberation and to reasserting over them a radical hegemony that pretends to universality in its command of theory (or of a reified notion of culture) but is in fact no less local and particularistic in its origins. To return to the question of the culture of the local: rather than predefined, cultures of resistance must themselves emerge in the course of struggles for the integrity of local community, for its livelihood, and for its democratic aspirations. However difficult, or even impossible, these aspirations may be in the face of the daily ravaging of life, there is little about them that is cause for disdain.

Any agenda of liberation originating in any one source, if it is to remain true to its goals of liberation, can only take the form of general propositions for local consideration (or, conversely, local propositions for general consideration) rather than binding axioms formulated in accordance with teleological presuppositions or, its opposite, the reification of local cultures. When capital is flexible, can radical resistance to it afford to be rigid and one dimensional? In the concluding chapter, I offer some reflections on these problems that are intended not as solutions, but as propositions that might be worth considering in thinking through the problem of liberation.

Women, Ecology, Science

Vandana Shiva, a physicist by training, is director of the Research Foundation for Science, Technology, and Natural Resource Policy in Dehradum, India, and a member of the Third World Network based in Kuala Lumpur, Malaysia. She is active in policymaking bodies, such as the United Nations, as well as in citizens' movements, of which the Chipko (Tree-hugging) movement of northern India is the most prominent. She is a foremost advocate of biodiversity. She writes: *

The parochial roots of science in patriarchy and in a particular class and culture have been concealed behind a claim to universality, and can be seen only through other traditions—of women and non-Western peoples. . . . The myth that the "scientific revolution" was a universal process of intellectual progress is being steadily undermined by feminist scholarship and the histories of science of non-western cultures. These are relating the rise of the reductionist paradigm with the subjugation and destruction of women's knowledge in the west, and the knowledge of non-western cultures. . . . I characterise modern western patriarchy's special epistemological tradition of the "scientific revolution" as "reductionist" because it reduced the capacity of humans to know nature both by excluding other knowers and other ways of knowing, and it reduced the capacity of nature to creatively regenerate and renew itself by manipulating it as inert and fragmented matter. Reductionism has a set of distinctive characteristics which demarcates it from all other non-reductionist knowledge systems which it has subjugated and replaced. The basic ontological and epistemological assumptions of reductionism are based on homogeneity. It sees all systems as made up of the same basic constituents, discrete, unrelated and atomistic, and it assumes that all basic processes are mechanistic. The

* Vandana Shiva, Staying Alive: Women, Ecology and Development (London: ZED Books, Ltd., 1988). I am indebted to Roxann Prazniak for acquainting me with this book and Shiva's work in general. Indeed, this essay has benefited much from Roxann's own insights into the problems discussed.

mechanistic metaphors of reductionism have socially reconstituted nature and society. In contrast to the organic metaphors, in which concepts of order and power were based on interconnectedness and reciprocity, the metaphor of nature as a machine was based on the assumption of separability and manipulability. . . . This domination is inherently violent, understood here as the violation of integrity. . . . Uniformity allows the knowledge of parts of a system, to be taken as knowledge of the whole. Separability allows context-free abstraction of knowledge and creates criteria of validity based on alienation and non-participation, then projected as "objectivity." "Experts" and "specialists" are thus projected as the only legitimate knowledge seekers and justifiers [pp. 21–23]. . . . In December 1987, two prizes were awarded in Stockholm: the Nobel Prize for Economics was given to Robert Solow of MIT for his theory of growth based on the dispensability of nature. In Solow's words, "The world can, in effect, get along without natural resources, so exhaustion is just an event, not a catastrophe." At the same time, the Alternative Nobel Prize (the popular name for the Right Livelihood Award), instituted "for vision and work contributing to making life more whole, healing our planet and uplifting humanity," honoured the women of the Chipko movement who, as leaders and activists, had put the life of the forests above their own and, with their actions, had stated that nature is indispensable to survival [p. 218].

5

Borderlands Radicalism

Borderlands

In her *Borderlands/La Frontera*, the Chicana lesbian author Gloria Anzaldua writes: "The new *mestiza* copes by developing a tolerance for contradictions, a tolerance for ambiguity. She learns to be Indian in Mexican culture, to be Mexican from an Anglo point of view. She learns to juggle cultures. She has a plural personality, she operates in a pluralistic mode—nothing is thrust out, the good, the bad and the ugly, nothing rejected, nothing abandoned. Not only does she sustain contradictions, she turns the ambivalence into something else."[64]

The writer of these lines lives in the borderlands, the literal borderlands of national boundaries as well as the metaphorical borderlands of social categories. In the age of flexible production, we all live in the borderlands. Capital, deterritorialized and decentered, establishes borderlands where it can move freely, away from the control of states and societies but in collusion with states against societies. Anzaldua's border between the United States and Mexico is also the site of the Maquiladora industries in which global capital flourishes off the cheap labor of Mexican laborers (mostly women), free from unions, pollution controls, and social responsibilities, blessed by the government of Mexico for bringing in technologies and jobs, encouraged by the United States government for guaranteeing the health of transnational corporations.

Maquila industries are but one form of "special economic zones," privileged spaces for the global motions of capital through which governments around the world put themselves on the pathways of transnational capital while sustaining the fiction of national sovereignty and development. Regions within nations, sometimes entire nations, seek to make themselves into free trade zones; free for capital, that is, with those left outside its motions free only to consume the products of capital if they can afford to do so. Borderlands take over from centers, and life is to be lived out as one endless conjuncture of different times and different spaces. Ambivalence is the condition of life, but what is the "something else" into which it may be turned?

One of the many revolutions of capitalism has been to transform subject-object relationships, and with it, the question of theory. The same capitalism that objectified the Other in order to justify its global conquest, having incorporated the Other into the world of capitalism, has no choice but to recognize co-presence to all within its domain. As Clifford Geertz has put it: "The end of colonialism altered radically the nature of the social relations between those who ask and look and those who are asked and looked at. The decline of faith in brute fact, set procedures, and unsituated knowledge in the human sciences, and indeed in scholarship generally, altered no less radically the askers' and lookers' conception of what it was they were trying to do."[65]

Just as the emergence of formerly colonial societies out of "cultural invisibility" (in Renato Rosaldo's words)[66] has led to a proliferation of subject positions, so it has forced out into the open the internal complexity of the individual subject who occupies a position *between* societies, with all the contradictory pluralities of such a situation. Again to quote Geertz:

> The transformation, partly juridical, partly ideological, partly real, of the people anthropologists mostly write about, from colonial subjects to sovereign citizens, has (whatever the ironies involved in Uganda, Libya, or Kampuchea) altered entirely the moral context

within which the ethnographical act takes place. Even those exemplary elsewheres—Levi-Strauss' Amazon or Benedict's Japan—that were not colonies, but stranded hinterlands or closed-off empires "in the middle of the sea," stand in a quite different light since Partition, Lumumba, Suez, and Vietnam changed the political grammar of the world. The more recent scattering of encapsulated peoples across the globe—Algerians in France, Koreans in Kuwait, Pakistanis in London, Cubans in Miami—has only extended the process by reducing the spacing of variant turns of mind, as has, of course, jet-plane tourism as well. One of the major assumptions upon which anthropological writing rested until only yesterday, that its subjects and its audience were not only separable but morally disconnected, that the first were to be described but not addressed, the second informed but not implicated, has fairly well dissolved. The world has its compartments still, but the passages between them are much more numerous and much less secured.[67]

The result is summarized by Renato Rosaldo: "A renewed concept of culture thus refers less to a unified entity ('a culture') than to the mundane practices of everyday life. . . . Ethnographers look less for homogeneous communities than for the border zones within and between them. Such cultural border zones are always in motion, not frozen for inspection."[68]

This predicament describes the dominant cultural/theoretical paradigm, or paradigms, that go under the name of "postmodernism." Post-modernism, articulating the condition of the globe in the age of flexible production, has done great theoretical service by challenging the tyrannical unilinearity of inherited conceptions of history and society. The political price paid for this achievement, however, has been to abolish the subject in history, which destroys the possibility of political action, or to attach action to one or another diffuse subject positions, which ends up in narcissistic preoccupations with self of one kind or another.

Having broken down subject positions implicit in teleological social categories (such as classes, genders, ethnicities, etc.), the task is now to reconstitute the subject once again in accordance with new radical visions. If "guerilla marketeers" can break down subjectivities in order to reconstitute people around the world as consuming subjects, radical critics of capitalism can do no less. So far, the former would seem to have an advantage over the latter. "Guerilla marketeers" know what they want of the world. Radical critics, deprived of the anchorage of past visions, mostly feed off one another and involute deeper and deeper into the realms of signs, fantasies, bodies, whatever.

The borderlands are the condition of life at the present. What kind of subject positions are possible in the borderlands? The question is impossible to answer in the abstract because the borderlands are by definition ambiguous and full of contradictions. More importantly, no two borderlands are identical. The reconstitution of the subject, under the circumstances, can only be local and conditional, produced not out of a priori theoretical categories but in the course of multi-faceted struggles against oppression and hegemony.[69] If I may rephrase Anzaldua, genders, classes, ethnicities are not "roles" that exist independently of one another, or as aggregates of social categories, but the constituents of the same subjectivity or of social groups. They may be reconstituted differently under different circumstances, but reconstituted they must be if they are to serve a purpose other than expressing different modes of alienation. Repudiation of the abstractions of capital is the first indispensable step to this end. Reaffirmation of a common humanity and of human bonds with nature, where the modern and the post-modern may have much to relearn from the premodern, is the indispensable goal, however "soft" it may seem as a vision in its theoretical "primitivism." In between, on the way to the vision, it is necessary to face squarely those problems that account for the "co-suffering" of which Nandy speaks, the recognition of which is less avoidable than at any time in the past because, for all the diversity of circumstances, we as much as they live in the borderlands.

Postcoloniality

Post-modernism parodies what it set out to criticize by contributing to the destruction of public responsibility, even to the notion of a public, rendering politics into a "politics of identity." The parody turns without notice into complicity in the ideological consolidation of the social, political, and cultural relationships produced by Global Capital.

This predicament is cogently illustrated by an offshoot of post-modernism that has acquired prominent visibility in recent years —the so-called postcolonial discourse or theory.[70] Postcolonial discourse is particularly pertinent to the discussion here for two reasons. First, though its putative target is the legacy of colonial discourses in general, it is especially concerned to challenge earlier radical critiques of colonialism and oppression—in particular, Marxism. Secondly, postcolonial discourse is global in its compass and in the questions it raises which are quite similar to the questions under discussion here. Unlike other "post"-marked words, postcolonialism claims as its special provenance the terrain that in an earlier day used to go by the name of "Third World." It is intended, therefore, to achieve an authentic globalization of cultural discourses by extending the intellectual concerns and orientations that have originated at the central sites of EuroAmerican cultural criticism and by introducing into the latter the voices and subjectivities from the margins of earlier political and/or ideological colonialism, which now demand a hearing at the center.

One enthusiastic promoter of "postcolonial discourse," Gyan Prakash, enunciates its major themes cogently in the following statement:

> One of the distinct effects of the recent emergence of postcolonial criticism has been to force a radical re-thinking and re-formulation of forms of knowledge and social identities authored and authorized by colonialism and western domination. For this reason, it has also created a ferment in the field of knowledge. This is not to

say that colonialism and its legacies remained unquestioned until recently: nationalism and marxism come immediately to mind as powerful challenges to colonialism. But both of these operated with master-narratives that put Europe at [their] center. Thus, when nationalism reversing Orientalist thought, attributed agency and history to the subjected nation, it also staked a claim to the order of Reason and Progress instituted by colonialism; and when marxists pilloried colonialism, their criticism was framed by a universalist mode-of-production narrative. Recent postcolonial criticism, on the other hand, seeks to undo the Eurocentrism produced by the institution of the west's trajectory, its appropriation of the other as History. It does so, however, with the acute realization that postcoloniality is not born and nurtured in a panoptic distance from history. The post-colonial exists as an aftermath, and after—after being worked over by colonialism. Criticism formed in the enunciation of discourses of domination occupies a space that is neither inside nor outside the history of western domination but in a tangential relation to it. This is what Homi Bhabha calls an in-between, hybrid position of practice and negotiation, or what Gayatri Chakravorty Spivak terms catachresis; "reversing, displacing, and seizing the apparatus of value-coding." [71]

To elaborate on these themes: (1) postcolonial criticism repudiates all master-narratives and, since the most powerful current master-narratives are Eurocentric—the products of post-Enlightenment European constitution of history—takes the criticism of Eurocentrism as its central task. (2) Foremost among these master-narratives to be repudiated is the narrative of modernization, both in its bourgeois and its Marxist incarnations. Bourgeois modernization ("developmentalism") represents the renovation and redeployment of "colonial modernity . . . as economic development." [72] Marxism, while it rejects bourgeois modernization, nevertheless perpetuates the teleological assumptions of the latter by framing inquiry in a narrative of modes of production, in which postcolonial history appears as a transition (or an aborted transition) to capitalism. [73] Repudiation of the narrative of modes of production, it needs to be added, does not necessarily mean the repudiation of Marxism, for postcolonial criticism acknowledges a strong Marxist inspiration.[74]

(3) Needless to say, Orientalism, in its constitution of the colony as Europe's Other in which the Other is reduced to an essence without history, must be repudiated. But so must nationalism, which, while challenging Orientalism, has perpetuated the essentialism of Orientalism (by affirming a national essence in history) as well as its procedures of representation.[75] (4) Repudiation of master-narratives is necessary to dispose of the hegemonic Eurocentric assumptions built into those master-narratives that have been employed in the past to frame Third World histories. It is necessary also to resist all spatial homogenization and temporal teleology, thus requiring the repudiation of all "foundational" historical writing. According to Prakash, a foundational view assumes "that history is ultimately founded in and representable through some identity—individual, class, or structure—which resists further decomposition into heterogeneity."[76] The most significant conclusion to follow from the repudiation of "foundational" historiography is the rejection of capitalism as a "foundational category" on the grounds that "we cannot thematize Indian history in terms of the development of capitalism and simultaneously contest capitalism's homogenization of the contemporary world."[77] (Obviously, given the logic of the argument, any Third World country could be substituted here for India.)

(5) "Post-foundational history," in its repudiation of essence and structure and simultaneous affirmation of heterogeneity, also repudiates any "fixing" of the "third-world subject" and, therefore, of the Third World as a category:

> The rejection of those modes of thinking which configure the third world in such irreducible essences as religiosity, underdevelopment, poverty, nationhood, non-Westernness . . . unsettles the calm presence that the essentialist categories—east and west, first world and third world—inhabit in our thought. This disruption makes it pos-

sible to treat the third world as a variety of shifting positions which have been discursively articulated in history. Viewed in this manner, the Orientalist, nationalist, Marxist and other historiographies become visible as discursive attempts to constitute their objects of knowledge, that is, the third world. As a result, rather than appearing as a fixed and essential object, the third world emerges as a series of historical positions, including those that enunciate essentialisms.[78]

It is noteworthy here that, along with the repudiation of capitalism and structure as "foundational categories," there is no mention in the above statement of a capitalist structuring of the world, however heterogeneous and "discrepant" the histories within it, as a constituting moment of history. (6) Finally, post-foundational history approaches "third-world identities as relational rather than essential."[79] Post-foundational history (which is also postcolonial history) shifts attention from "national origin" to "subject position."

[Consequently,] the formation of third-world positions suggests engagement rather than insularity. It is difficult to overlook that all the third-world voices identified in this essay, speak within and to discourses familiar to the "West" instead of originating from some autonomous essence, which does not warrant the conclusion that the third-world historiography has always been enslaved, but that the careful maintenance and policing of East-West boundaries has never succeeded in stopping the flows across and against boundaries and that the self-other opposition has never quite been able to order all differences into binary opposites. The third world, far from being confined to its assigned space, has penetrated the inner sanctum of the first world in the process of being "third-worlded"—arousing, inciting, and affiliating with the subordinated others in the first world. It has reached across boundaries and barriers to connect with the minority voices in the first world: socialists, radicals, feminists, minorities.[80]

To underline the affirmations in the above statement, which are quite representative of the postcolonial stance on contemporary

global relations (and of its claims to transcending earlier conceptualizations of the world): (1) attention needs to be shifted from
national origin to subject position, hence a "politics of location"
takes precedence over politics informed by fixed categories (in this
case, the nation, but quite obviously referring also to categories
such as Third World and class, among others); (2) though First/
Third World positions may not be interchangeable, they are nevertheless quite fluid, which implies a necessity of qualifying, if not
repudiating, binary oppositions when articulating their relationship; (3) local interactions take priority over global structures in
the shaping of these relationships, which implies that they are best
comprehended historically in their heterogeneity than structurally
in their "fixity"; (4) these conclusions follow from the "hybrid-
ness" or "in-betweenness" of the postcolonial subject, which is not
to be contained within fixed categories or binary oppositions; and,
(5) since postcolonial criticism has focused on the postcolonial
subject to the exclusion of an account of the world outside of the
subject, the global condition implied by postcoloniality appears at
best as a projection of postcolonial subjectivity and epistemology.
In other words, a discursive constitution of the world aligned with
the constitution of the "postcolonial" subject must take place,
much as earlier the world was constituted by the epistemologies
that are now the object of "postcolonial" criticism.

"Postcolonialism" has been described as "a dislocating discourse that raises theoretical questions regarding how dominant
and radical theories 'have themselves been implicated in the long
history of European colonialism—and, above all, the extent to
which [they] continue to determine both the institutional conditions of knowledge as well as the terms of contemporary institutional practices—practices which extend beyond the limits of the
academic institution.' " [81] Against these practices, "postcolonialism" asserts the "primacy of a politics of difference and struggle,"
but without the reification of difference into oppositions that pre-
suppose fixed subject positions. The "cultural politics of difference," according to Cornel West, presupposes a need "to trash
the monolithic and homogeneous in the name of diversity, multi-

plicity, and heterogeneity; to reject the abstract, general, and universal in light of the concrete, specific, and particular; and to historicize, contextualize and pluralize by highlighting the contingent, provisional, variable, tentative, shifting, and changing." [82]

The politics of difference, it seems fair to conclude, is a politics of location and identity where both the nature of the struggle and the struggling subject itself are contingent, contradictory, and complex. Such subjects are "border crossers," capable of occupying multiple subject positions because they are complex and contradictory in their own constitution and are "engaged in an effort to create alternative public spheres." [83]

The promoters of postcolonial discourse attribute its rapidly acquired popularity to its effectiveness in remedying or transcending the deficiencies of earlier radical criticism. I would like to suggest, to the contrary, that postcolonial discourse resonates with the ideological demands of a world situation under Global Capitalism, which accounts for its popularity not just among self-styled radicals but among the managers of global capital as well. The reasons may be indicated briefly; they will also help distinguish the position I take here from that assumed by postcolonial discourse, which is necessary since much of what I have written above overlaps with important aspects of the postcolonial argument:

1. Postcolonialism, in making Eurocentrism into the primary object of criticism, diverts attention from contemporary problems of oppression and inequality to focus on the legacy of the past. Power appears in postcolonial discourse as residual power and, because of the emphasis on culture (Eurocentric metanarratives), as something to be disposed of by cultural criticism. By denying to capitalism "foundational" status, the postcolonial argument also suppresses the generation of new forms of power, of oppression and inequality, under contemporary capitalism. Multiculturalism is postcolonialism's answer to Eurocentrism. This postcolonial "solution" to the problem of global inequality coincides with the ideology of Global Capitalism, which, transnational in its operations, can no longer afford the cultural Eurocentrism of a bygone

day when the centers of global capital were still territorialized in Europe and North America.

2. In its denial of a capitalist structuring of the world (hence, of colonialism and neo-colonialism, of the three worlds, etc.), in its insistence on fragmentation and the primacy of local encounters, in its repudiation of unified subjectivity and "binarism" in favor of "hybridity" and "multiculturalism," and in its affirmation of fluid relations and transposable subject positions, postcolonial discourse often reads very much like a description of life under Global Capitalism. Yet the postcolonial argument offers these phenomena as the keys to liberation rather than as manifestations of new forms of oppression, dislocation, and alienation. It also projects these phenomena back into the past to call into question the legacy of colonialism, to shift the burden of "underdevelopment" onto the "underdeveloped" themselves, and, in the name of historicity (against structure), to erase from historical consciousness the memory of oppression and inequality so that the past is abolished as a source of critical perspectives on the present. Here, too, postcolonialism coincides with the ideology of Global Capitalism, which seeks to abolish distinctions between "Us and Them" and perceives the persistence of "vestigial memory" as the greatest obstacle to dealing with the present.[84] In either case, the contradictions of modernism are erased to yield a modernization that identifies the future with current modernity.

3. Postcolonialism stresses the "borderlands" as opposed to fixed identities, which may account for the proliferation of works with "border" in their titles in recent years as postcolonial discourse has achieved a pervasive presence in cultural criticism. Borderlands provide locations for the "politics of difference," for the mutual articulation of cultures and subjectivities. But in much of postcolonial criticism, borderlands appear in ahistorical and metaphorical guise. Borderlands may appear on the surface as locations of equal cultural exchange, but they are products of historical inequalities, and their historical legacy continues to haunt them. To reflect on my own previous statement that "we all live in the borderlands," it is necessary to underline that we do not all live in the same borderlands and that the affirmation of difference does not imply that all differences are equal.[85] As long as drastic inequality persists, the cultural exchanges that take place across unequal positions, too, must bear upon them the mark of inequality—except for those between groups and classes (such as the "transnational capitalist class") that have achieved some semblance of transnational homogeneity and equality, who can laud their own "multiculturalism" while turning a blind eye to all those marginalized by their success. This inequality, moreover, is not metaphorical or merely a legacy of past cultural attitudes but a product of the continuing operations of capital. The argument here, too, stresses the "borderlands," but borderlands that are the very product of the operations of global capital. Maquiladoras and special economic zones are the paradigms of "borderlands," which exist not to promote equal exchange but to render the exploitation of labor more effective. If borderlands as they are presently constituted liberate anyone, it is capital. Hence borderlands point not to liberated zones but to zones that pose new problems for the task of liberation and may at best serve as points of departure, not as points of arrival.

4. Postcoloniality (like post-modernity) calls for fluid subject positions; so does Global Capitalism. Guerilla marketeers seek to reconstitute subjectivity on a daily basis to adjust consumers to the marketing needs of ever new products. Capital demands flexibility from labor—to adjust to flexible working times in accordance with the needs of production, to be prepared to shift from one kind of work to another as production demands, and, therefore, to "retool" constantly, to "remake" themselves so they can adjust to flexible production. The "death of the subject" finds its production parallel in the "death of the worker." Karl Marx drew a distinction between "working to live" and "living to work" to distinguish alienated from non-alienated labor. Under alienated labor, he wrote, the laborer "related to the *product of his labor* as to an *alien* object," which also alienated the laborer from his/her

"species-being." The result: "He is at home when he is not working, and when he is working he is not at home." [86] Marx believed in
the dignity of work, in work as a mark of human "species-being."
Capital has been trying since its beginnings to liberate itself from
laborers by de-skilling the worker to make him/her as close as possible to an appendage to a machine, and it has now come close
to achieving this goal as well. The laborer who can retool daily
is a laborer that mimics production, so that alienated labor itself
ceases to have any meaning as a critical concept. Reich's "routine
production" and service workers require few skills beyond the
ability to follow "routines"; the "symbolic-analysts" command
great skills still—to manipulate and to dislocate, themselves no
less than the markets for their products. Viewed "up" from the
processes of production and consumption, the post-modern argument for fluid subject positions loses the benign visage it presents
in the realm of cultural criticism and appears for what it is: the
fetishization of alienation.

   5. The problem presented by postcolonial discourse, then, may
be summarized as a problem of liberating discourse that divorces
itself from the material conditions of life, in this case Global Capitalism as the "foundational" principle of contemporary society
globally. Intended as a critique of ideology, it becomes itself an
ideological articulation of a contemporary situation. Its critical
edge is directed at radical positions of the "past," while as far
as capitalism is concerned it at best blunts criticism, at worst in-
corporates into its own utopia the social consequences of Global
Capitalism. It ignores (or disguises) the fact that the "multiple,
complex, and contradictory" subject positions of the borderlands
nevertheless assume coherence and direction (if only temporarily)
according to context, so that the analysis of the context becomes
of primary significance—which it by-passes, presumably because
that kind of analysis smacks too much of Marxism. Also ignored
is the location of "postcolonial discourse"—First World academic institutions in which "postcolonial intellectuals" themselves
occupy privileged positions as members of a transnational intellec-

tual class, as much a product of global capitalism as the transnational capitalist class. Global Capitalism has jumbled up notions of space and time. It has also jumbled up political positions so that it is not uncommon these days to find "radicals" sounding like ideologues of power.

Contradiction, Overdetermination, Theory, and History: Marxism as Hermeneutic

. . . One must not treat all the contradictions in a process as being equal but must distinguish between the principal and secondary contradictions, and pay special attention to grasping the principal one. But, in any given contradiction, whether principal or secondary, should the two contradictory aspects be treated as equal? Again, no. In any contradiction the development of the contradictory aspects is uneven. Sometimes they seem to be in equilibrium, which is however only temporary and relative, while unevenness is basic. Of the two contradictory aspects, one must be principal and the other secondary. The principal aspect is the one playing the leading role in the contradiction. The nature of a thing is determined mainly by the principal aspect of a contradiction, the aspect which has gained the dominant position.

But this situation is not static; the principal and the non-principal aspects of a contradiction transform themselves into each other and the nature of the thing changes accordingly. In a given process or at a given stage in the development of a contradiction, A is the principal aspect and B is the non-principal aspect; at another stage or in another process the roles are reversed—a change determined by the extent of the increase or the decrease in the force of each aspect in its struggle against the other in the course of the development of a thing.[87]

Mao was concerned primarily with Marxist categories such as bourgeois and proletariat, colonialism and anticolonialism, capitalism and feudalism, and he sought to resolve contradictions in accordance with Marxist teleology. Disassociated from teleology and opened up to other categories, contradictions offer a hermeneutic of social relations as they appear under different historical contexts, are different therefore as relationships, and, because they are constituted differently, do not lend themselves to reconstitution in identical (homogeneous) ways; the relationships, in their particularity, historicize the categories of social analysis themselves:

> It is so with all opposites; in given conditions, on the one hand they are opposed to each other, and on the other they are interconnected, interpenetrating, interpermeating and interdependent, and this character is described as identity. In given conditions, all contradictory aspects possess the character of non-identity and hence are described as being in contradiction. But they also possess the character of identity and hence are interconnected. How can [opposites] be identical? Because each is the condition for the other's existence.[88]

Where identity is overdetermined, homogenization can be achieved only by coercion—or ideological manipulation. Mao recognized this and proceeded to ignore it. The Guomindang Marxist Tao Xisheng argued on one occasion that if Marxism is truly scientific, Marxist analysis should yield different results when applied to different circumstances. He used the example of chemical analysis. Chemical analysis of water yields one set of elements, he observed, of salt, a different set.[89]

Freud's concept of "overdetermination," Laplanche and Portalis explain, suggests that "formations of the unconscious [and, therefore, of subjectivity] can be attributed to a plurality of factors," which can be understood in different ways: "(a) the formation in question is the result of several causes, since one alone is not sufficient to account for it, and (b) the formation is related to a multiplicity of unconscious elements which may be organised in different meaningful sequences, each having its own coherence at a particular level of interpretation." Multiple causes, they further remark, imply neither an infinity of interpretations nor "independence, or parallelism" of different meanings for the same phenomenon.[90]

The concept of "overdetermination" offers a way of grasping the problem of ideology and of political struggles that more than ever take the form of struggles over ideology. An overdetermined subjectivity is of necessity unique (since it is grounded in individual experiences that, by definition, cannot replicate themselves in identical ways); it is for the same reason ambiguous. Social categories intersect at the level of individual subjectivity, where they shape or condition one another, may reinforce the practices they inform, but also introduce contradictions into those practices: a proletarian is never just a proletarian, a woman is never just a woman, a Chinese person is never just a Chinese, to name a few such categories. A "Chinese proletarian woman" has a coherence at one level of analysis; at another, Chineseness, proletarianness and womanhood may appear as contradictory endowments. "Ambiguity is dispelled by context," Laplanche and Portalis say.[91] The context shapes how the "unconscious elements" are "organised in a meaningful sequence" by bringing forward one or another category as the organizing principle for the others; just as Mao's "principal contradiction" (or "principal aspect of a contradiction") shapes the field of contradictions.[92] The principal contradiction, however, is neither transparent nor is it determinable a priori from theory; rather, it is contextual and, therefore, historical and must be uncovered with the aid of theory.

In his *Freud for Historians*, Peter Gay writes:

> Overdetermination is in fact nothing more than the sensible recognition that a variety of causes—a variety, not infinity—enters into the making of all historical events, and that each ingredient in historical experience can be counted on to have a variety—not infinity—of functions. The historian, working with a wealth of causal agents subtle and gross, immediate and remote, intent on scanting none of them and on subjecting them to order, can only agree and

applaud. Seek complexity, the historian and the psychoanalyst can say in unison, seek complexity and tame it.[93]

The operative phrase is "tame it," which leaves ambiguous whether the historian discovers the order in the situation or *orders* the complex situation, the latter placing the historian firmly into the situation being explained. Mao's idea of revolutionary practice specified that theory must at all times confront concrete actuality, with the revolutionary intermediating the process. Theory was thus rendered into a hermeneutic, a tool of interpretation (can much the same be said of psychoanalysis?).[94]

It is also clear from the case of Mao and the Chinese revolution, however, that the interpreting subject is also the ideologizing subject. Ideology presupposes the restructuring of many individual subjectivities in parallel configurations on a stable basis to render ambiguous, unstable, and contextual subjectivities into social categories; so that individual consciousness may be forged into the consciousness of social groups. Just as guerilla marketeers seek to understand "local" cultures in order to forge out of them a homogeneous consumer culture, Mao the revolutionary sought to understand differences in consciousness so as to condense them into a homogeneous class consciousness, just as he sought to re-order complex social relationships to render them simple.

Marxist theorists have long understood and enunciated the problematic nature of ideology. Antonio Gramsci's concept of hegemony was itself an acknowledgment of the uncertain relationship between social existence and ideological position: that the worker did not automatically have a worker's consciousness by virtue of being a worker. Consciousness had to be shaped culturally and in the process of political activity so that revolutionary hegemony could replace bourgeois hegemony.[95] Louis Althusser pointed to the same problem, in his notion of "ideological state apparatuses," from another direction. An overdetermined consciousness could be given direction only institutionally, through family, educational, and cultural apparatuses that consolidated ideology across social divides to secure existing power relations culturally. There, too, the conclusion seems clear enough: Revolutionaries must counter the "ideological state apparatuses" of the bourgeoisie with their own to consolidate *their* power.[96]

The problem, of course, is that hegemony is hegemony whether it is revolutionary or not, and the goal of liberation is to abolish hegemony, not to perpetuate it. Indeed, the greatest obstacle to liberation may not be hegemony of one kind or another but the very inability to imagine life without hegemony. As the Italian anarchist Malatesta put it on one occasion:

> Someone whose legs have been bound from birth but had managed nevertheless to walk as best he could, might attribute his ability to move to those very bonds which in fact serve only to weaken and paralyse the muscular energy of his legs.
>
> If to the normal effects of habit is then added the kind of education offered by the master, the priest, the teachers, etc., who have a vested interest in preaching that the masters and the government are necessary; if one were to add the judge and the policeman who are at pains to reduce to silence those who might think differently and be tempted to propagate their ideas, then it will not be difficult to understand how the prejudiced view of the usefulness of, and the necessity for, the master and the government took root in the unsophisticated minds of the labouring masses.
>
> Just imagine if the doctor were to expound to our fictional man with the bound legs a theory, cleverly illustrated with a thousand invented cases to prove that if his legs were freed he would be unable to walk and would not live, then that man would ferociously defend his bonds and consider as his enemy anyone who tried to remove them.[97]

Anarchists have been consistent in the critique of hegemony; they have also been the least successful of all radicals in dealing with questions of power. Hence the dilemma: Without homogeneity, political struggle may be impossible; homogenization, however, reintroduces ideology—and hegemony. What does this dilemma say about politics?

Sites of Struggle: The Global and the Local in Contemporary Radicalism

To recapitulate briefly: (1) Capital, more pervasive than ever within Global Capitalism, is very much a "foundational" principle of contemporary life. Any discourse of liberation worthy of the name must address the problems of material and social existence that it presents. (2) To the extent that capital commands a formative presence globally, Marxism is as relevant as ever to the analysis of the world. The fall of existing socialist states, rather than point to "the death of Marxism," frees Marxism from its servitude to bureaucratic modernizationism. Especially relevant are the ideas of class, for class formations are becoming genuinely global, and of "totality," which is more necessary than ever to "cognitive mapping" as the operations of capital reach unprecedented levels of mystification. (3) The totality to which I refer is a nonreductionist totality, which makes room for social concepts and categories that have not been particularly prominent in Marxist analyses of the past. Radical analysis must take as its point of departure "overdetermination" as a fundamental characteristic of social existence and consciousness and must resist the reductionism that is implicit in the sublating of alternative categories into a single, "totalistic" category—in the case of Marxism, class. Gender, ethnicity, and race are fundamental in shaping social existence and consciousness and must enter any discourse of liberation as primary considerations. Radical analysis must resist the teleology of concepts as much as the teleology of a modernizationist spatiality and temporality, and it must allow for nontotalizing solutions even as it confronts totality as a contemporary problem. This openness also means allowing for consideration of "utopian" solutions. Theory is essential to analyzing contemporary life, but theory does not point the way to the future except as an account of the constraints that need to be overcome to imagine alternative futures. Recognizing diversity and historicity may call for the abolition of theory, which is of necessity homogenizing and totalizing. (4) Liberation is not a theoretical but an ethical proposition, just as the aspiration for a humane existence is not a privilege but a right. It does not follow that the struggle for liberation is arbitrary, without any constraints on it. The complexity and fluidity of subjectivity that is implicit in the currently pervasive metaphor of "borderlands" implies not arbitrary voluntarism but "overdetermination" of subjectivity. The recognition of this complexity is liberating, but only given the simultaneous recognition that an overdetermined subjectivity has contextual direction and preference; in other words, the subject is still a subject in everyday existence, regardless of what any wild theorizing may suggest.[98] The problem that faces the quest for liberation is to create non-hegemonic subjectivity that still has the integrity to pursue the quest for liberation. Imagining alternative futures, under the circumstances, is not an act but a process; a constant negotiation between conflicting demands on the future to emerge from the struggle for liberation, that struggle to overcome obstacles to a humane existence.

Under the circumstances, where is resistance to capitalism to be located, and what might be the nature of the resistance? Along with "borderlands," another term has acquired prominent visibility in recent radical criticism: "local." I think it important here briefly to think out its implications.

Rachael Kamel, representing the American Friends Service Committee, recently wrote a book called *The Global Factory*, significantly subtitled, *Analysis and Action for a New Economic Era*.[99] The book is interesting as a counterpoint to Reich's *The Work of Nations*. The analytical premises are the same, Global Capitalism; but unlike the latter, which seeks to forget the past and adjust the United States to the new era, Kamel remembers the past and seeks ways to preserve the existence and dignity of "routine production workers" in the United States and elsewhere. She does so with a clarity that contrasts strikingly with the obscurantism of discussions about the "local" in the cultural criticism of academic intellectuals (if this sounds "anti-intellectual," so be it). She describes the plight of workers (mostly working women) in the United States, the Maquiladoras, and the Philippines, as they are played off against one another by transnationals, and suggests several ways of coordinating resistance. Kamel writes:

> Each of the projects we have described may seem tiny, especially when contrasted to the size and power of transnational corporations. Yet each is also a small step toward building a movement that could bring together hundreds of local grassroots campaigns, within the United States and internationally.
>
> At this writing, the idea of a broad-based, multinational movement to tackle the problems of the global factory is still a vision. What we have tried to document in this guide is that the global factory is composed of thousands of concrete local situations—and that each of us, whatever setting we live and work in, can take small, accessible actions to confront our specific situations.
>
> By understanding that every local story is part of a global "big picture," we can open up space for dialog [sic] and sharing of experiences—especially across barriers of language, nationality, gender, race and class. And as that process of communication moves toward networking and coalition-building, the vision of a multinational movement can become a reality.[100]

From the tree-hugging women of northern India to the women workers of the Maquiladora industries, from indigenous people's movements seeking secession from colonialist states (most recently in Hawaii) to the western Kansas counties that wish to secede from Kansas and the United States because they feel abused by governments, local movements have emerged as a pervasive phenomenon of the contemporary world. These movements are not simply a symptom of conventional localism but a response to the motions of global capital (and its attendant political and social consequences): The local has emerged as the site of resistance as capitalism, in its manipulation of local differences, has brought the local to the surface of consciousness. The assimilation of the local to the global, which is another way of saying the homogenization of the world socially and culturally, points to the local as the location for resistance to capital as well.

The affirmation of the local and, therefore, of diversity thus defined is not without its own problems, as activists such as Kamel and Vandana Shiva are well aware. One such problem is in the celebration of premodern pasts, which, in the name of resistance to the modern and the rationalist homogenization of the world, results in a localism or a "third-worldism" that is willing to overlook past oppressions out of a preoccupation with capitalist or Eurocentric oppression, which in the name of the recovery of spirituality affirms past religiosities that were themselves excuses for class and patriarchal inequalities. One consequence of Global Capitalism is that there are no longer any local societies that have not been worked over already by capital and modernity; insistence on local "purity" may well serve as an excuse for a reactionary revival of older forms of oppression, as women in particular have been quick to point out in India and among the indigenous people's movements in North America.[101] The local is valuable as a site for resistance to the global, but only to the extent that it also serves as the site of negotiation for abolishing inequality and oppression inherited from the past, which is a condition of any promise it may have for the future. It is neither possible nor desirable to dismiss the new awareness that is the product of modernity as just another trick of Eurocentrism.

What this discussion points to is a "critical localism," which, even as it subjects the present to critical evaluation from past perspectives, retains in the evaluation of the past the critical perspectives afforded by modernity. Excluded from this localism are romantic nostalgias for communities past, hegemonic nationalist yearnings of a new kind (as with the so-called Confucian revival in East Asia), or historicisms that would imprison the present in the past. An example of the latter are well-intentioned but misguided efforts in recent scholarship on China to produce a "China-centered" view of history. The effort is well-intentioned because it seeks to rescue Chinese history from its subjection to the hegemony of EuroAmerican teleologies and concepts; but it is misguided because it is accompanied by assertions that the Chinese themselves are incapable of producing this history because they have been tainted by Western concepts and, therefore, have lost touch with their own past. Such efforts, which deny to the Chinese contemporaneity while giving born-again EuroAmericans the privilege of interpreting China's past for the Chinese, are reminiscent of nineteenth-century Europeans who, claiming historicalness for themselves while denying it to others, appropriated the meaning of history for the whole world, especially for the Third World.[102] At the other extreme is that ethnocentrism in the critique of hegemony, that, in its preoccupation with EuroAmerican conceptual and theoretical hegemony, falls into affirmations of pre-Western ethnicities and spiritualities, without accounting for the problem of oppression in general, which has not been the monopoly of the West or of capitalism even though it may have been carried to unprecedented levels in the modern world in its denial of alternative modes of existence. The dilemmas faced by today's liberation struggles against EuroAmerican and capitalist oppression, I believe, should not be evaded by sweeping under the rug premodern forms of oppression. As a first cut, it is necessary to distinguish between stateless communities (or communities where state organization and local community coincided, such as tribal organizations around the world)[103] and communities that provided excuses for far-flung state organizations, as in the premodern empires of China, India, and the Ottoman Empire. The former are easier to sympathize with, the latter, much less so, since their reinvocation of premodern pasts, however anti-hegemonic in terms of their relationship to the West, barely disguises national chauvinisms of a new kind. The Confucian revival, for instance, is not unrelated to arguments for a "Greater Chinese" economic region.

These two positions are quite different in their sources and implications. It is also important to distinguish EuroAmericans speaking for Third World pasts from those of Third World peoples speaking for their own pasts in an effort to rescue their identities from "death by assimilation" (in the words of the writer, Frank Chin). Nevertheless, both positions are problematic; it is not only silly to deny the undeniable—that economic and cultural conjunctures during the past century have defined the conditions of existence for non-European or American peoples—but also socially (as distinct from politically) reactionary to ignore past forms of oppression that have been brought to the forefront of historical consciousness by these conjunctures. It is the continued existence of such forms of oppression, compounded and overdetermined now by new forms of oppression, that makes Marxist and gender analyses in particular as relevant as ever to critical understanding.

The local as I use it here has meaning only inasmuch as it is a product of the conjuncture of structures located in the same temporality but with different spatialities, which is what gives rise to the problem of spatiality and, therefore, of the local in the first place. The conjunctural situation also defines the culture of the local, which is stripped of its reification by daily confrontation between different cultures and appears, instead, in the nakedness of its everyday practice. Under conditions of isolation and stability, culture appears timeless in its daily reproduction (if such is ever entirely the case), but the conjunctural situation reveals culture as an activity of production and ceaseless reconstruction. That culture is thus constantly constructed does not imply that the present is, therefore, immune to the burden of the past, only that the burden itself is restructured in the course of present activity. Neither does it mean that the past is unimportant; it only underlines the claims of the present, of the living, on the past rather than the other way around. Culture is no less cultural for being subject to change through the "practise of everyday life" (the term is Michel deCertau's), of which it is as much source as product. It is the prevalence of cultural conjuncture as a condition of life globally that has brought forth the sharp consciousness of culture as an on-going construction of everyday practice. This new awareness has been illuminated in the works of Pierre Bourdieu and Marshall Sahlins, who have argued out the implications for culture and history of conjunctures between past and present, between different social and cultural structures (which problematize the relationship between different presents as well as between the present and the past), and even between structure and event, especially when the event is of an unprecedented nature such as the contact of non-European peoples with Europeans.[104]

The immediate question here is what this ongoing construction of culture implies in terms of the resistance of the local to the global. Ashis Nandy has written that

> when two cultures of unequal secular power enter into a dialogue, a new hierarchy inevitably emerges, unless the dialogue creates a shared space for each participant's distinctive, unstated theory of the other cultures or, in its absence, each participant's general theory of culture. The concept of cultural relativism, expressed in the popular anthropological view that each culture must be studied in terms of its own categories, is limited because it stops short of insisting that every culture must recognize the way it is construed by other cultures. It is easy to leave other cultures to their own devices in the name of cultural relativism, particularly if the visions of the future of these other cultures have already been cannibalized by the worldview of one's own. It is less easy to live with an alien culture's estimate of oneself, to integrate it within one's selfhood and to live with that self-induced inner tension. It is even more difficult to live with the inner dialogue within one's own culture which is triggered off by the dialogue with other cultures because, then, the carefully built cultural defences against disturbing dialogues—and against the threatening insights emerging from the dialogues—begin to crumble.[105]

Nandy's view of cultural dialogue has been inspired by the approach to culture of Mohandas Gandhi who, Richard Fox tells us in his recent illuminating study of Gandhi, believed that "cultures change through collective experiments,"[106] experiments that use the present as their point of departure but that are open to diverse pasts in their pursuit of "truth." The local, I would like to suggest here, is the site for such experimentation. The "experimentation," however, has to be global in compass. Resistance that seeks to re-affirm some "authentic" local culture by ignoring the conjunctures that produced it is condemned to failure, if only because the so-called authentic local culture is daily disorganized by the global forces (e.g., guerilla marketeers) that seek to reconstitute it, to assimilate it into global homogenization.

This assimilation of the local is the second, more serious, problem with the local as a strategic concept of resistance. Through assimilation, different localities become pawns in the hands of global capital in its guerilla warfare against societies globally. This problem may, indeed, be the most serious challenge facing resistance/liberation movements in our day: how to deal with global companies that, at the least sign of interference with their activities (be they labor demands or efforts to restrict the harm they inflict on local societies and ecologies), threaten to pick up and move to new localities, which new technologies enable them to do (more accurately, mobility is the major goal of developing new technologies). How does resistance deal with a General Motors that holds entire communities and cities in suspense while shutting down production plants, waiting to see the outcome of communities competing with one another by offering better and sweeter deals to the corporation to keep it in their respective communities to save jobs—and the livelihood of the entire community? Local resistance, under the circumstances, if it is to be meaningful at all, must be translocal both in consciousness and in action—a big "if," and possibly cause for a widespread sense of futility globally. The dilemma is heightened by the fact that local consciousness, which is necessary as the basis for resistance, contradicts the translocal activity and consciousness that is a necessity of successful resistance. If this contradiction is overcome, however, the very fragmentation of the globe by capital may be turned into an advantage for resistance movements: The demand for the authentically local against its exploitation as a means to assimilation may "overload" global capitalism, driving *it* to fragmentation.[107]

Besides the part the local may play in resistance to Global Capitalism, Henry Giroux has provided a suggestive means for the local to serve as a building block for the future. Giroux's "border pedagogy" is derivative of post-modern/postcolonial "politics of difference." Dissatisfied, however, with the affirmation of difference as an end in itself, which he rightly perceives to be subversive of meaningful politics, he seeks ways to formulate new kinds of "unity in diversity"[108] that may serve as grounds for "nontotalizing politics."[109] Especially important is his idea of "formative narratives," which cogently expresses the considerations I have suggested above. His explanation of this idea provides an appropriate conclusion to this essay:

> The postmodern attack on totality and foundationalism is not without its drawbacks. While it rightly focuses on the importance of local narratives and rejects the notion that truth precedes the notion of representation, it also runs the risk of blurring the distinction between master narratives that are monocausal and formative narratives, that provide the basis for historically and relationally placing different groups or local narratives within some common project. To draw out this point further, it is difficult to imagine any politics of difference as a form of radical social theory if it doesn't offer a formative narrative capable of analyzing difference within rather than against unity.[110]

NOTES

1. "The Invention of TimeSpace Realities: Towards an Understanding of our Historical Systems," in Immanuel Wallerstein, *Unthinking Social Science: The Limits of Nineteenth Century Paradigms* (London: Polity Press, 1991), pp. 135–48.
2. "The Changing Function of Historical Materialism," in George Lukacs, *History and Class Consciousness: Studies in Marxist Dialectics*, trans. by Rodney Livingstone (Cambridge, MA: The MIT Press, 1971), pp. 223–25, 229.
3. "Duke Faculty on Marxism," *The Missing Link* (March 1992): 5.

4. "Science and Ideology," in Paul Ricoeur, *From Text to Action: Essays in Hermeneutics, II*, trans. by Kathleen Blamey and John B. Thompson (Evanston, IL: Northwestern University Press, 1991), pp. 246–69, quotation on 259.

5. For an example, see Gilbert Rozman, "Theories of Modernization and Theories of Revolution: China and Russia," in *Symposium on the Modernization of China, 1860–1949* (Taipei: Academic Simca, 1991), pp. 633–46.

6. I owe the notion of "derivative discourse" to Partha Chatterjee, *Nationalist Thought and the Colonial World—A Derivative Discourse* (London: ZED Books, 1986).

7. Ricoeur, *Text to Action*, p. 260.

8. Karl Marx and Friedrich Engels, *Manifesto of the Communist Party*, in *The Marx-Engels Reader*, ed. by Robert C. Tucker (New York: W. W. Norton & Co., 1972), pp. 331–62, quotation on 339.

9. Ibid., pp. 336–39, *passim*.

10. Ibid., p. 338.

11. "History of the Opium Trade" (*The Times*, 27 September 1850) in K. Marx and F. Engels, *Collected Works*, vol. 16 (New York: International Publishers, 1981), p. 16.

12. Karl Marx, *Capital*, vol. 1. Quoted in *Karl Marx: Selected Writings in Sociology and Social Philosophy*, trans. and ed. by T. B. Bottomore (New York: McGraw-Hill Book Co., 1956), p. 112.

13. *The Marx-Engels Reader*, p. 331.

14. Ibid., p. 338.

15. *Late Marx and the Russian Road; Marx and "the Peripheries of Capitalism": A Case Presented by Theodor Shanin* (New York: Monthly Review Press, 1983).

16. I use this terminology instead of the more common "sinification of Marxism" because the latter implies the absorption of Marxism into a Chinese cultural sphere, whereas what Mao had in mind, I have argued at length elsewhere, was the production of a new kind of Marxism and a new kind of "Chineseness" out of the articulation of Marxist theory with the material and subjective circumstances of contemporary China. See Dirlik, "The Predicament of Marxist Revolutionary Consciousness: Mao Zedong, Antonio Gramsci, and the Reformulation of Marxist Revolutionary Theory," *Modern China* 9, no. 2 (April 1983): 105–32.

17. The discussion below draws on my *Revolution and History: The Origins of Marxist Historiography in China, 1919–1937* (Berkeley, CA: University of California Press, 1978). Also relevant to the discussion is my "Marxism and Chinese History: The Globalization of Marxist Historical Discourse and the Problem of Hegemony in Marxism," *Journal of Third World Studies* 4, no. 1 (Spring 1987):151–64.

18. James Wilkinson, *Intellectual Resistance in Europe*, quoted in Chang-tai Hung, *War and Popular Culture: Symbols, Images and Languages of Resistance in Modern China, 1937–1945*, forthcoming. This latter work provides a fine illustration of the confrontation between abstractions and social actualities from the perspective of art and literature.

19. The discussion below draws on my "Mao Zedong and 'Chinese Marxism,'" forthcoming, *The Encyclopedia of Asian Philosophy* (Routledge).

20. A fine illustration of such use of concepts is to be found in Mao Zedong's *Report from Xunwu*, trans. (with an Introduction and Notes) by Rogert R. Thompson (Stanford, CA: Stanford University Press, 1990). The implications of this report are drawn out by Roxann Prazniak in her review essay of this report. See Prazniak, "The Art of Folk Revolution," in *Peasant Studies* 17, no. 3 (Spring 1990):195–206.

21. Maurice Meisner has been the foremost interpreter of Mao as a populist Marxist. See, for example, his "Utopian Socialist Themes in Maoism," in *Peasant Rebellion and Communist Revolution in Asia*, ed. by J. W. Lewis (Stanford, CA: Stanford University Press), pp. 207–52.

22. Wallerstein, *Unthinking Social Science*.

23. In the discussion here, my ideas of "flexible production" and its implications for the world economy have been informed by the following works: F. Frobel, J. Heinrichs, and O. Kreye, *The New International Division of Labor* (Cambridge, G.B.: Cambridge University Press, 1980); David Harvey, *The Condition of Post-Modernity* (Cambridge, MA: Basil Blackwell, 1989); Fredric Jameson, "Post-Modernism: The Cultural Logic of Late Capitalism," *New Left Review* 146 (July/August 1984):53–92; Ernest Mandel, *Late Capitalism* (London and New York: Verso Books, 1987); Claus Offe,

Disorganized Capitalism (Cambridge, MA: The MIT Press, 1985); Michael J. Piore and C. F. Sabel, *The Second Industrial Divide: Possibilities for Prosperity* (New York: Basic Books, 1984); Robert B. Reich, *The Work of Nations* (New York: Alfred A. Knopf, 1991); Robert J. S. Ross and Kent C. Trachte, *Global Capitalism: The New Leviathan* (Albany, N.Y.: State University of New York Press, 1990); Leslie Sklair, *Sociology of the Global System* (Baltimore: The Johns Hopkins University Press, 1991).

24. E. H. Carr, "A Historical Turning Point: Marx, Lenin, Stalin," in *Revolutionary Russia*, ed. by Richard Pipes (Cambridge, MA: Harvard University Press, 1968), pp. 282–94.

25. Samir Amin, *Delinking: Towards a Polycentric World* (London and New Jersey: ZED Books, 1990); S. Amin, G. Arrighi, A. G. Frank, and I. Wallerstein, eds., *Dynamics of Global Crisis* (New York: Monthly Review Press, 1982).

26. Marie Lavigne, *International Political Economy and Socialism*, trans. by David Lambert (Cambridge, G.B.: Cambridge University Press, 1991), p. 354.

27. Ibid., p. 65.

28. Quoted in ibid., p. 65.

29. Kazimierz Z. Poznanski, *Technology, Competition, and the Soviet Bloc in the World Market* (Berkeley, CA: Institute of International Studies Research Series, no. 70, 1987), pp. 90–122, 206–10. The problem of technology in Soviet relations with the world, as perceived by Soviet policymakers historically, is discussed in detail by Bruce Parrott, *Politics and Technology in the Soviet Union* (Cambridge, MA: The MIT Press, 1983). Significant changes in Soviet thinking from the seventies are discussed in Erick P. Hoffman and Robbin F. Laird, *Technocratic Socialism: The Soviet Union in the Advanced Industrial Era* (Durham, NC: Duke University Press, 1985).

30. Lavigne, *International Political Economy*, p. 361.

31. *Time*, 8 December 1980, p. 23. Similar sentiments were expressed in a US Committee on Foreign Affairs report, *Winning the Cold War: The U.S. Ideological Offensive* (1964): "In foreign affairs, certain objectives can be better achieved through direct contact with the people of foreign countries than with their governments. Through the intermediary of the techniques and instruments of communica-

tions, it is possible today to reach important and influential sectors of the population of other countries, to inform them, to influence their attitudes, and maybe to succeed in motivating them to certain determined actions. These groups, in turn, are capable of exercising considerable pressure on their governments." Quoted in Leslie Sklair, *The Sociology of the Global System* (Baltimore: The Johns Hopkins University Press, 1991), p. 136.

32. For Trilateralist views of the world, see Holly Sklar, ed., *Trilateralism: The Trilateral Commission and Elite Planning for World Management* (Boston: South End Press, 1980).

33. See the works cited in note 23. For special examples, see Jeffrey Henderson, *The Globalisation of High Technology Production* (London: Routledge, 1991); James Lardner, "The Sweater Trade," *New Yorker* (11 and 18 January 1988); Gary Gereffi, "Global Sourcing and Regional Divisions of Labor in the Pacific Rim," in *What is in a Rim? Critical Perspectives on the Asia-Pacific Idea*, ed. by Arif Dirlik (Boulder, CO: Westview Press, 1993).

34. Immanuel Wallerstein, "Development: Lodestar or Illusion?" in *Unthinking Social Science*, pp. 104–24, 109–10.

35. Riccardo Petrella, "World City-States of the Future," *NPQ* (*New Perspectives Quarterly*) (Fall 1991):59–64. See also, "A New Hanseatic League?" *New York Times*, 23 February 1992, E3.

36. Kenichi Ohmae, "Beyond Friction to Fact: The Borderless Economy," *NPQ* (Spring 1990):20–21.

37. For an early discussion of this problem, see Raymond Vernon, *Sovereignty at Bay: The Multinational Spread of US Enterprises* (New York: Basic Books, 1971). Robert B. Reich in the United States and Kenichi Ohmae in Japan have emerged in recent years as the most articulate spokesmen for the view that nation-states are on their way out in the new global organization of the economy. See Reich, *The Work of Nations* (New York: Alfred A. Knopf, 1991); and Ohmae, *The Borderless Economy: Power and Strategy in the Interlinked Economy* (New York: Harper Business, 1990). *The Harvard Business Review* is an important forum for and, in general, a promoter of this position. The view that nation-states are in decline has its challengers: See, for example, James Fallows' review of Lester Thurow's *Head to Head: The Coming Economic Battle Among Japan, Europe and America* (*The New York Review of Books* 39, no. 8 [23 April

1992]:12–17). In accepting the views of the former, I realize, there is a danger of falling into what may be an ideological position. But there is considerable corroborating evidence from different ideological positions (see note 23); and it is possible to state, without qualms about ideology, that there is a dynamic force at work in the world system that was not there before or was there in a much weaker and powerless form.

38. Xiangming Chen, "New Spatial Division of Labor and Commodity Chains in the Emerging Greater China Economic Region," paper presented at the PEWS XVI (Political Economy of the World System) Conference, Duke University (16–18 April 1992); Dali Yang, "China Adjusts to the World Economy: The Political Economy of China's Coastal Development Strategy," *Pacific Affairs* 64, no. 1 (Spring 1991):42–64; David Zweig, "Internationalizing China's Countryside: The Political Economy of Exports from Rural Industry," *The China Quarterly* 128 (December 1991):716–41.

39. "Sulian zhengbian hou Zhonggode xianshi yingdui yu zhanlue xuanze" ("A Realistic Response and Choice of Strategy in the Aftermath of Political Changes in the Soviet Union") in *Zhongguozhi chun* (*China Spring*) (January 1992):35–39.

40. Ibid., pp. 38–39.

41. Dali Yang, "China Adjusts." The recent National People's Congress (March–April 1992) reaffirmed the commitment of the state to this mode of development. For a discussion of the importance of special economic zones and how much China may have to learn in this regard from the history of capitalism, see Fang Sheng, "Duiwai kaifang he liyong ziben zhuyi" ("Opening to the Outside and Using Capitalism"), *Renmin ribao* (*People's Daily*), 23 February 1991. See also Deng Xiaoping's observations on the flourishing economy of south China (Guangdong) during his visit there in, "Deng Xiaoping nanxun shide Jianghua" ("Deng Xiaoping's Talks during His Visit to the South), *Zhongguozhi chun* (*China Spring*) (April 1992):14–15.

42. Kenichi Ohmae, "Beyond Friction to Fact." See also, James Gardner, "Global Regionalism," *NPQ* 9, no. 1 (Winter 1992):58–59.

43. For origins of the "three worlds," see the very illuminating essay by Carl E. Pletsch, "The Three Worlds, or the Division of Social Scientific Labor, circa 1950–1975," *Comparative Studies in Society and History* 23, no. 4 (December 1981):565–90.

44. Wallerstein, "Development: Lodestar or Illusion?" p. 113. Petrella

guesses that around 4 billion of the world's population (the portion left out of the high-tech Hanseatic League) is in a hopeless situation. *NPQ* (Fall 1991):59–64. For the impoverishment of the population in the most modernized country in the world, the United States, see Reich, *The Work of Nations*, chapter 16.

45. Jameson, "Post-Modernism: The Cultural Logic of Late Capitalism."

46. Harvey, *The Condition of Post-Modernity.*

47. Lyotard, *The Post-Modern Condition: A Report on Knowledge,* trans. by Geoff Bennington and Brian Masumi (Minneapolis: University of Minnesota Press, 1984), p. xxiv.

48. Wallerstein, *The Modern World-System* (New York: Academic Press, 1974–1989); Fernand Braudel, *The Perspective of the World,* vol. 3 of *Civilization and Capitalism,* trans. by Sian Reynolds (New York: Harper and Row, 1984).

49. Wallerstein, "Marx and Underdevelopment" and "Marxisms as Utopias: Evolving Ideologies," in *Unthinking Social Science,* pp. 151–84.

50. Thompson, *The Making of the English Working Class* (New York: Vintage Books, 1966); James C. Scott, *Weapons of the Weak: Everyday Forms of Peasant Resistance* (New Haven: Yale University Press, 1985).

51. From a conference on marketing held at the Research Triangle Park, North Carolina, 27 February 1987. Quoted in Rick Roderick, "The Antinomy of Post-modern Bourgeois Thought," paper presented at the Marxism and Society seminar, Duke University, March 1987 (14 pp.), pp. 1–2. Quoted with the author's permission.

52. See, for example, Mao's meticulous "mapping" of social relations and structure in the *Report from Xunwu.* The classic statements on Chinese guerilla warfare are to be found in *Selected Works of Mao Tse-tung,* vol. 1 (Peking: Foreign Languages Press, 1965).

53. "The Logic of Global Business: An Interview with ABB's Percy Barnevik," *Harvard Business Review* (March–April 1991), pp. 90–105, quotation on 95. For detailed discussion of corporate responses to organizational problems, see Stanley M. Davis, *Managing and Organizing Multinational Corporations* (New York: Pergamon Press, 1979), especially pp. 231–49: "Trends in the Organization of Multinational Corporations," by Davis.

54. Ohmae, "Beyond Fiction to Fact."

55. "The Logic of Global Business," p. 105.
56. The term is from Felix Guattari and Toni Negri, *Communists Like Us: New Spaces of Liberty, New Lines of Alliance*, trans. by Michael Ryan (New York: Semiotext(e) Foreign Agents Series, Columbia University, 1990), p. 22.
57. Lester Thurow in *Head to Head*, cited in *NPQ* 9, no. 1 (Winter 1992):41–45. How oxymoronic this term is may be gleaned from the interview in the same issue of *NPQ* with Lee Kuan Yew, the foremost promoter of "Confucian capitalism" as the former prime minister of Singapore (described by *NPQ* as "the grand old man of Asia"). The interview does not even raise the question that there might be a significant difference between "community," as generally understood, and the fascist homogenization of society in Singapore, which, judging by Singapore's success, provided capital with a late twentieth-century Shangri-la. Not all Chinese, or East Asians, needless to say, subscribe to these authoritarian interpretations of Confucianism and community. On the other hand, it is probably not coincidental that Deng Xiaoping recently "picked out Singapore as a model not only of an economic miracle, but also of strict social control." Catherine Sampson, "Chinese turn from conflict to capitalism," *The London Times*, 3 June 1992, p. 10.
58. For specific references, see my discussion of "postcolonialism" below.
59. Ernesto Laclau writes: "Abandoning the myth of foundations does not lead to nihilism, just as uncertainty as to how an enemy will attack does not lead to passivity. It leads, rather, to a proliferation of discursive interventions and arguments that are necessary, because there is no extra-discursive reality that discourse might simply reflect. Inasmuch as argument and discourse constitute the social, their open-ended character becomes the source of a greater activism and a more radical libertarianism. Humankind, having always bowed to eternal forces—God, Nature, the necessary laws of history—can now, at the threshold of postmodernity, consider itself for the first time the creator and constructor of its own history." Laclau, "Politics and the Limits of Modernity," in *Universal Abandon? The Politics of Postmodernism*, ed. by A. Ross (Minneapolis: University of Minnesota Press, 1988), pp. 79–80. Also quoted in Henry Giroux, *Border Crossings: Cultural Workers and the Politics of Education* (New York and London: Routledge, 1992), p. 54.

60. For "cognitive mapping," see Fredric Jameson, "Cognitive Mapping," in *Marxism and the Interpretation of Culture*, ed. by Cary Nelson and Lawrence Gossberg (Urbana and Chicago: University of Illinois Press, 1988), pp. 347–57.
61. Sklair, *Sociology of the Global System*, pp. 52–84.
62. See the global survey of managers in Rosabeth Moss Kanter, "Transcending Business Boundaries: 12,000 World Managers View Change," *Harvard Business Review* (May–June 1991):151–64.
63. Reich, *The Work of Nations*, pp. 171–84.
64. Gloria Anzaldua, *Borderlands/La Frontera: The New Mestiza* (San Francisco: Spinsters/aunt lute, 1987), p. 79.
65. Clifford Geertz, *Works and Lives: The Anthropologist as Author* (Stanford, CA: Stanford University Press, 1988), pp. 131–32.
66. Renato Rosaldo, *Culture and Truth: The Remaking of Social Analysis* (Boston: Beacon Press, 1989), p. ix. Rosaldo, in turn, derives the concept from Adrienne Rich.
67. Geertz, *Works and Lives*, p. 132.
68. Rosaldo, *Culture and Truth*, p. 217.
69. For a lengthier discussion, see Arif Dirlik, "Culturalism as Hegemonic Ideology and Liberating Practice, *Cultural Critique* 6 (Spring 1987):13–50.
70. For an elaboration of the comments below on "postcolonialism," see Arif Dirlik, "The Postcolonial Aura: Third World Criticism in the Age of Global Capitalism," *Critical Inquiry*, 20.2 (Winter 1994): 328–56.
71. Gyan Prakash, "Postcolonial Criticism and Indian Historiography," *Social Text* 31/32:8–19, quotation on 8. I use Prakash's discussions of "postcoloniality" here because he has made the most systematic attempts at accounting for the concept and also because his discussions bring to the fore the implications of the concept for historical understanding. As this statement reveals, Prakash himself draws heavily for inspiration on the characteristics of "postcolonial" consciousness delineated by others, especially by Homi Bhabha who has been responsible for the prominence in discussions of postcoloniality of the vocabulary of "hybridity" and other specialized terms. Bhabha's work, however, is responsible for more than the vocabulary of postcolonialism, for he has proven himself to be something of a master of political mystification and theoretical obfuscation, of reducing social and political problems to psychological ones, and of substi-

tuting post-structuralist linguistic manipulation for historical and social explanation—which show up in much of postcolonial writing but rarely with the same virtuosity (and incomprehensibleness) that he brings to it. For some of his more influential writings, see "Of Mimicry and Man: The Ambivalence of Colonial Discourse," *October* 28 (1984):125–33; "The Commitment to Theory," in *Questions of Third World Cinema*, ed. by Jim Pines and Paul Willemen (London: BFI Publishing, 1989), pp. 111–32; "The Other Question: Difference, Discrimination and the Discourse of Colonialism," in *Literature, Politics and Theory*, ed. by F. Barker, P. Hulme, I. Iversen, and D. Loxley (London and New York: Methuen, 1986), pp. 148–72; and his essays in Homi Bhabha, ed. *Nation and Narration* (London and New York: Routledge, 1990). Bhabha is a prime example of the Third World intellectual who has been completely reworked by the language of First World cultural criticism.

72. Prakash, "Writing Post-Orientalist Histories of the Third World: Perspectives from Indian Historiography," *Comparative Studies in Society and History* 32, no. 2 (1990):383–408, quotation on 393.

73. Ibid., p. 395. See also Dipesh Chakrabarty, "Post-coloniality and the Artifice of History: Who Speaks for 'Indian' Pasts?" *Representations* 37 (Winter 1992):1–26, especially p. 4.

74. Prakash, "Postcolonial Criticism," p. 14–15. See also, Spivak, *The Post-Colonial Critic: Interviews, Strategies, Dialogues*, ed. by Sarah Harasym (New York and London: Routledge, 1990).

75. Parakash, "Post-Orientalist Histories," pp. 390–91.

76. Ibid., p. 397.

77. Prakash, "Postcolonial Criticism," p. 13.

78. Prakash, "Post-Orientalist Histories," p. 13.

79. Ibid., p. 399.

80. Ibid., p. 403.

81. Robert Young, quoted in Giroux, *Border Crossings*, p. 20.

82. Cornel West, "The New Cultural Politics of Difference," *October* 53 (Summer 1990):93. Also quoted in Giroux, *Border Crossings*, p. 20.

83. Giroux, *Border Crossings*, pp. 21–22.

84. Reich, *The Work of Nations*, pp. 5, 154–68.

85. I am grateful to Maivan Lam, who commented on an earlier version of this section, for the point that we may all be in the borderlands but that someone in my position is hardly in the same borderlands as a "black man suffering from AIDS on the streets of New York."

86. Karl Marx, *The Economic & Philosophic Manuscripts of 1844*, ed. with an Introduction by Dirk J. Struik (New York: International Publishers, 1964), pp. 106–27, quotation on 110.
87. Mao Zedong, "On Contradiction," in *Selected Works of Mao Tse-tung*, vol. 1 (Peking: Foreign Languages Press, 1965), p. 333.
88. Ibid., p. 338.
89. Tao Xisheng, "Shehui kexue jiangzuo" (Symposium on Social Science), *Xin shengming (New Life)* 2, no. 5 (May 1929):1.
90. Jean Laplanche and J. B. Portalis, *The Language of Psychoanalysis*, trans. by Donald Nicholson-Smith (New York: W. W. Norton & Co., 1973), pp. 292–93.
91. Ibid., p. 292.
92. This aspect of Mao's thought was recognized early on by Louis Althusser. See Althusser's "Contradiction and Overdetermination," in *For Marx* (New York: Vintage Books, 1970), pp. 89–128.
93. Peter Gay, *Freud for Historians* (New York: Oxford University Press, 1985), p. 187.
94. Mao, "On Practise," in *Selected Works of Mao Tse-tung*, vol. 1, pp. 295–309.
95. For Gramsci's idea of hegemony, see Chantal Mouffe, "Hegemony and Ideology in Gramsci," in *Gramsci and Marxist Theory*, ed. by C. Mouffe (London: Routledge & Kegan Paul, 1979), pp. 168–204.
96. Althusser, "Ideology and Ideological State Apparatuses," in *Lenin and Philosophy and Other Essays* (New York and London: Monthly Review Press, 1971), pp. 127–86.
97. Errico Malatesta, *Anarchy* (London: Freedom Press, 1984), p. 12.
98. For a timely, and devastating, critique of theory that has turned the "real world" into "fable," see Christopher Norris, *Uncritical Theory* (Amherst: The University of Massachusetts Press, 1992).
99. Rachael Kamel, *The Global Factory: Analysis and Action for a New Economic Era* (American Friends Service Committee, 1990).
100. Ibid., p. 75.
101. Meera Nanda, "Is Modern Science a Western, Patriarchal Myth? A Critique of the Populist Orthodoxy," *South Asia Bulletin* 11, nos. 1 & 2 (1991):32–61.
102. For a seminal and influential work arguing this position, see Paul Cohen, *Discovering History in China* (New York: Columbia University Press, 1984).
103. For an excellent account of indigenous people's movements and

their relationship to existing states, see Maivan Lam, "The Age of Association: The Indigenous Assertion of Self-determination at the United Nations," unpublished manuscript, cited with the author's permission.

104. Pierce Bourdieu, *The Logic of Practice* (Stanford, CA: Stanford University Press, 1990), for a recent explication of his views; and Marshall Sahlins, *Islands of History* (Chicago: University of Chicago Press, 1985).

105. Ashis Nandy, *Traditions, Tyranny and Utopias: Essays in the Politics of Awareness* (Delhi: Oxford University Press, 1987), pp. 16–17.

106. Richard G. Fox, *Gandhian Utopia: Experiments with Culture* (Boston: Beacon Press, 1989), p. 26.

107. This notion of "overloading the system" as a means of resistance I owe to Wallerstein, "Development: Lodestar or Illusion?" p. 124. What I have in mind here may be illustrated by an episode from South Pacific culture. In his analysis of oral traditions in the South Pacific, Subramani observes that South Pacific writers have, "in some instances, rediscovered their oral literatures by reading translations of them by European researchers." The goal of European researchers in undertaking this kind of activity around the globe, at least initially, was to understand the natives to better control, convert, or assimilate them. With a new cultural consciousness that aims at liberation, these same "researches" now serve the cause of liberation and the assertion of local identity against assimilation. Subramani, *South Pacific Literature: From Myth to Fabulation* (Suva: History of the South Pacific, 1985), p. 32.

108. Giroux, *Border Crossings*, p. 79. For "unity in diversity," see Yuji Ichioka, " 'Unity within Diversity': Louis Adamic and Japanese-Americans," Duke University, Working Papers in Asian/Pacific Studies, no. 1 (1987).

109. Giroux, *Border Crossings*, p. 79.

110. Ibid., p. 54.

INDEX

University Press of New England
publishes books under its own imprint and is the publisher for Brandeis University Press, Brown University Press, University of Connecticut, Dartmouth College, Middlebury College Press, University of New Hampshire, University of Rhode Island, Tufts University, University of Vermont, Wesleyan University Press, and Salzburg Seminar.

About the Author
Arif Dirlik is Professor of History at Duke University and author of *Anarchism in the Chinese Revolution* (1991) and *The Origins of Chinese Communism* (1989).

Library of Congress Cataloging-in-Publication Data
Dirlik, Arif.
 After the revolution: waking to global capitalism / Arif Dirlik.
  p.   cm.
 Includes bibliographical references and index.
 ISBN 0–8195–5274–7.—ISBN 0–8195–6279–3 (pbk.)
  1. Communism—History—20th century. 2. Capitalism—History—20th century. 3. Post-communism. I. Title.
HX40.D58 1994
335.43′0904—dc20   93–39490
♾